Also by the author:

Call My Name - The Baby Name Guide

MIND

Selwyn Michael Gishen

Published by G-Media

5020 NW24th Circle, Boca Raton
Florida, 33431

ISBN 978-0-6151-8140-0

Contents

Acknowledgements

"How should we live our lives"?

I believe that the most universal answer to this question can be found from the mystics of all the great religions and philosophies of the world, independent of ethnicity or culture.

The great sages throughout the eons have all provided the same simple message that is at once applicable to all of mankind and to each individual for all times. Here is their simple and profound formula.

Love! - Serve! - Meditate! - Realize!

Love is the synthesis of all diversity into a sense of empathy - the ability to feel and experience the oneness of the world; the unity in the diversity.

Service is the desire and willingness to help others to achieve their dreams *without* the need for compensation or reciprocity. The joy is in the giving and in the other person's happiness.

Meditation is the focus upon, and constant awareness of the perfect peace that is within and without each one of us, once we transcend the mind.

Realization is the direct experience of all three of the above ideals; the oneness of life, the joy in

11

service and the existence of a perfect peace When we realize, we experience the abundance that the universe provides and endows upon us. We experience that we are a note in the "one song" and that the "one song" vibrates through each and every one of us in an astounding harmony.

I acknowledge with deep humility all the teachers who have imparted such a profound and simple life formula.

I also gratefully acknowledge my own teachers and those with whom I am able to practice love, and to serve and to meditate, especially my wife Analisa and my two children, Kriya and Kayle.

Preface

A single human's potential is carried in a seed before he or she is born.

Just like the acorn that carries within it the code of all that is required to become an oak tree, but which requires the four conditions of nurturing to make it manifest, so it is with the person. For the acorn, these four conditions are: soil, sun, water and time.

The same is true for humankind. Seeds that are wanting of expression are just waiting to be fertilized, so that they can manifest. The purpose of manifestation is expressed through each human being, by means of an individual persona, which is the vehicle through which one's character is developed. And just like the acorn, the person needs certain nurturing conditions: a body, food and water, sunlight and time.

However, in the case of us humans, a more sophisticated faculty is available, which has evolved to manifest human potential. This faculty is called MIND.

Only a member of the human species can access the dual function of mind, and experience both the external world and the internal world for the purpose of using the experience as a deliberate act of self directed growth.

We only become aware of our potential by resolving the paradox of life. On the one hand, we are co-creators of a divine plan when we participate in life's drama, and on the other hand, life's drama is the experience that gives rise to an expansion of consciousness. So we create our world and we learn from it.

In accordance with our own individual code, we each act out a different expression of purpose. Such expression of purpose is really for our own personal realization of who we really are as creative spirit. It is in our creativity that we experience life's diversity and it is in the reflection of life's diversity that we learn to experience oneness.

The "mind" is a superb tool and faculty for both creating and reflecting our world to others while at the same time providing feedback to ourselves. With mind we have the ability to plan and to go forward. Yet we have the ability also to remember and look backward. This is the mind's usual functioning. It constantly travels between the past and the future. But we can also focus the mind deliberately. Just like a magnifying glass that focuses the sun's rays, we can burn a hole of light into the darkness that appears to surround us everywhere, by focusing on the present moment.

Hence mind is not only a tool or a faculty, which is necessary to function as a human, but it is also a tool for evolving the human condition to that of a higher order, through the act of free will.

All the seeds that we carry will eventually manifest into whom we must become as humans. Life will nurture such growth. Nature willl impose upon us the quality of our own seeds, which we ourselves constantly create, and which we carry with us, in the unconscious memory bank of our individual mind.

To help us navigate, and to keep in tune with the divine order of things, we are individually synchronized with a universal mind, for which we in society have a variety of names. These names are mostly taught to us by the conditioning factors of our environment, and our cultural and ethnic affiliations. The names are not important.

Although we are intimately connected to, and in sync with a universal mind, we have the capacity as individuals to respond and to act on the data that is gathered by the very act of being alive. This individual capacity is our "free will." And we are free to use it to either advance our evolution or to retard it. Such is the power of one's mind.

In this book we explore four underlying beliefs, born out of experience through the ages, and passed genetically through the human race, as a means and a mechanism for the evolution of our consciousness. As consciousness evolves, so do our physical vehicles. In the process of living, we can improve our situation by becoming aware of and harmonizing with the universal mind, as it is expressed through nature. By learning this harmony and by developing the mindset needed to focus our individual mind, we begin to function in terms of our true purpose as human beings. The joy of being human is in the process or the journey from birth to death. It is fully alive within us at each moment, if we can but reveal it.

The more we act to unify our humanity through internal action, the more the outside world will reflect back such a harmony to us and permit us the freedom to be totally unique as individuals. Each of us has a mission; to express ourselves as a note in a single song,

The word universe comes from Latin and means "One Song".

Mind

(according to Roget's New Millennium™ Thesaurus)

Main Entry: mind

Part of Speech: noun [1]

Definition: intelligence

Synonyms: *apperception, attention, brain, brainpower, brains*, capacity, cognizance, conception, consciousness, creativity, faculty, function, genius, gray matter, head, imagination, ingenuity, instinct, intellect, intellectual, intellectuality, intuition, judgment, lucidity, mentality, observation, perception, percipience, power, psyche, ratiocination, reason, reasoning, regard, sanity, sense, soul, soundness, spirit, talent, thinkbox, thinker, thought, understanding, wisdom, wits*

Main Entry: mind

Part of Speech: noun [2]

Definition: memory

Synonyms: *attention, cognizance, concentration, head, mark, note, notice, observance, observation, recollection, regard, remark, remembrance, subconscious, thinking, thoughts*

Main Entry: mind

Part of Speech: noun [3]

Definition: tendency

Synonyms: *attitude, belief, bent, conviction, desire, determination, disposition, eye, fancy, feeling, humor, impulse, inclination, intention, judgment, leaning, liking, mood, notion, opinion, outlook, persuasion, pleasure, purpose, sentiment, strain, temper, temperament, thoughts, tone, urge, vein, view, will, wish*

Main Entry: mind

Part of Speech: verb [1]

Definition: care

Synonyms: be affronted, be opposed, complain, deplore, disapprove, dislike, object, resent, take offense

Main Entry: mind

Part of Speech: verb [2]

Definition: comply

Synonyms: *adhere to, attend, behave, follow, follow orders, heed, keep, listen, mark, note, notice, obey, observe, pay attention, pay heed, regard, respect, take heed, watch*

Main Entry: mind

Part of Speech: verb [3]

Definition: tend

Synonyms: *attend, baby-sit, be attentive, behold, care for, dig, discern, discipline, ensure, give ears, govern, guard, listen up, look, make certain, mark, note, notice, observe, oversee, perceive, regard, see, sit, superintend, supervise, watch*

Main Entry: mind

Part of Speech: verb [4]

Definition: be careful

Synonyms: *be cautious, be concerned, be solicitous, be wary, take care, tend, trouble, watch.*

Main Entry: mind

Part of Speech: verb [5]

Definition: remember

Synonyms: *bethink, cite, recall, recollect, remind, reminisce, retain, retrospect, revive.*

Foreword

How changing your mind can change your life!

Millions of good, hard working honest people struggle to live and enjoy their lives. As the world becomes more and more densely populated, the conditions for survival seem to deteriorate. Water and food are scarcer each year. Resources are unevenly distributed and more than two thirds of the world's population now live below the standards of a civilized norm.

Nations are at war with each other, all in pursuit of a better standard of living. Religious zealots abound, each proclaiming their own superiority. Religion holds us prisoners of a faith that does not provide solutions. Schools don't teach us how to be happy. Parents, in most cases, teach their children the same things they were taught.

Myths perpetuate in the name of tradition, and family structure is disappearing because of social requirements and pressures. Governments are corrupt and the more they are relied upon to solve our problems, the more our problems increase.

We, as good intentioned souls, are trapped in a world of make believe. We have to make believe we are happy and that all is as it should be.

Sometimes in desperation, we do desperate things. We fight, we cry, and mostly we blame others. In our more sane moments, we laugh and we dance and we sing. When we are happy, we care for each other and the world takes on a different hue.

But it only lasts sporadically. That is why we need to do something to make it all different; and that requires each one of us to become a master of our own mind. If we want a life of 'abundance', then we must understand that we become what we deeply think and believe. If we think rich and believe we are rich, we can become rich, if we think and believe we are happy we can become happy. But it is not a question of creating positive thoughts and then achieving positive results. Quite honestly that doesn't work.

We need to develop a new mindset, one that has different patterns or habits. To do this we must have an open mind; one that is prepared to let go of old habits and replace them with new ones, which can only be developed by taking certain appropriate actions. We have to unlearn what we have learned. We need a philosophy that shapes the way we think. We need a formula that we can follow to keep us on the path each day until our new thinking becomes automatic.

Then we need to let direct experience become our true teacher. No one can tell us what sugar tastes like, we have to taste it for ourselves so that we can know for certain just what is the meaning of sweetness.

"Mind" is the recognition of an approach that will change our lives quickly, effectively and permanently. It is a methodology to bring into our lives whatever we can dream of and it is a universal teacher. The methodology works irrespective of race, creed, color, sex or religion. Those characteristics are all transcended. All we need to do is to change our focus from a self serving attitude to one of service through the Self, with a capital S. Another word for Self is Love. All we have to do is serve with love.

Is there any risk? The only risk is that we may find happiness and abundance, once we open ourselves to a mindset that attracts loving relationships, satisfying vocations and more laughter, singing and dancing.

To succeed in life, we have to take a chance and make a commitment. A small commitment can lead to a very large result. And there is no downside.

Read this book and apply the concepts. By finding abundance for ourselves, we make it available to others. Each of us has a purpose - to make this world a better place by making each of us a better person. Only we can do it!

How we think leads to how we *will act.*

The architect who sees a building in his mind's

eye, is performing an act of visualization. Then he draws the building on paper, in the finest of details. From that drawing, he measures the quantities of materials needed, and gives the information to the builder who in turn gathers the materials to finally erect the building.

The process from visualization to actualization *requires an act of free will*. We all have the power to direct <u>our</u> thinking *and only we can control our thoughts*. Therefore, how we think is how our world will appear for us and to us.

We are truly creators of *our* own world and, in partnership with the Universe we can and do create our own experiences.

The Universe supplies us with the necessary energy (the wind at our sails),which we use to create into thoughts and then process to create our very own world, either with or without abundance. It's up to us!

In the following poem, Eller Wilcox describes our two options in life............

One ship sails East

"But to every Soul there openeth,
A way, and a way, and a way,
A high soul climbs the high way,
And the low soul gropes the low,
And in between on the misty flats,
The rest drift to and fro.

But to every man there openeth,
A high way and a low,
And every mind decideth,
The way his soul shall go.

One ship sails East,
And another West,
By the self-same winds that blow,
'Tis the set of the sails
And not the gales,
That tells the way we go.

Like the winds of the sea
Are the waves of time,
As we journey along through life,
'Tis the set of the soul,
That determines the goal,
And not the calm or the strife".

Eller Wheeler Wilcox
(1850 -1919)

"Mind" Factors

Part 1 - The Preparation

We all want to achieve Health, Wealth, Wisdom, Love, and Freedom in our lives, but it is important to understand these terms in a deeper sense.

For instance, wealth is much more than money. Wealth is abundant living and abundant living has to do with fulfillment and contentment (peace of mind) and being satisfied with our life. Of course, wealth has something to do with money and the availability of money, when we need it. Hopefully, we do understand what real abundance is, and will apply this understanding to our daily lives and therefore, prosper on all levels.

The background philosophy and practical techniques revealed in this book will help you to attract abundance into your life. The way to do so is by developing a "new" mindset.

Each person on earth is a unique individual with talents and skills that he or she alone possesses. Each person is here to make a contribution to the world, in a unique and individual way.

No matter what our contribution is though, we need to understand that the universe requires each one of

us to make a purposeful contribution. Therefore, no matter what it is that we do contribute, we do so as an important part of a grand universal design.

Each person has his or her own special purpose and each person is special. Therefore, these lessons are for all of us. They are truths culled from the tree of life that grows throughout the ages and which offers its fruits, whenever we are ready to reach for them.

It is my sincere hope that the information in this book will serve you in a way that helps you to discover your own true purpose. If you already know and are living your purpose, then perhaps it will help you to manifest your purpose in such a way that you will be a shining light for others to heed and to follow.

For me, if only one person reads this information and benefits from it, and if the light goes on in his or her head, producing a moment of epiphany, then I have made a contribution to the world by passing on what I have been privileged to have learned.

I truly believe in the teaching that says, if you want your cup to be always filled, then you have to keep on emptying it.

In whatever way we can serve others, by doing so, we pour forth offerings from our cups, so that others may drink too. It is this pouring forth that makes space for our own cups to be constantly refilled. We will discover that the universe provides an infinite supply of abundance.

Preparing Our Mindset

The following four foundations are at the core of the understanding that is needed to reach the experience of truth; but before we can proceed, it is necessary to define "truth".

According to the American Heritage Dictionary, truth means;

> • the true or actual state of a matter: *He tried to find out the truth.*
>
> • conformity with fact or reality; verity: *the truth of a statement.*
>
> • a verified or indisputable fact, proposition, principle, or the like: *mathematical truths.*
>
> • the state or character of being true.
>
> • actuality or actual existence.
>
> • an obvious or accepted fact; truism; platitude.
>
> • honesty; integrity; truthfulness.
>
> • (*often initial capital letter*) ideal or fundamental reality apart from and transcending perceived experience: *the basic truths of life.*
>
> • agreement with a standard or original.

- accuracy, as of position or adjustment.

- Archaic. fidelity or constancy.

Now, I don't know about you, but I still don't know what is meant by the above defined "truth," even after reading all eleven definitions. I would also venture to say that the people who created those definitions also do not know.

For our purposes, let us redefine truth so that once and for all it is clear.

"Truth is that which never changes."

This is worth repeating.

"Truth is that which never changes."

So, if this definition of truth is correct, then we are immediately confronted with a large problem.

What is there that we can identify that does not change?

In fact, the only constant in life is change itself.

By definition then, *everything in creation must simply be a lie or an illusion!* But in what way then is life an illusion?

Because we *perceive* something to be truth, does not mean that it is truth. We might proclaim that it is truth, but that does not make it truth.

The following four principles of wisdom, when grasped properly, will change your mindset so radically that you will begin to see life differently.

Your 'perceptions' will be forever transformed. You will know your opinions to be "perceptions" and not to claim them as the "truth". This is the first step we need to take in order to grasp the "Mind" concept.

The Four Principles are:

- The Principle of "Cause and Effect"

- The Principle of Illusion or "Mind Fog"

- The Principle of a State of "Non Duality"

- The Principle of "Free Will"

The Principle of Cause and Effect
(known generally as the Law of Karma.)

The law of Karma – "action" is a scientific fact. For every action there is an equal and opposite reaction. Newton's third law states that forces occur in pairs, one called the **action** and the other the **reaction** (*actio et reactio* in Latin).

Such a force exists whenever humans take action to do something. Every action causes an impression in the "mind-stuff" within our being. These impressions are stored in our memories. Every action taken by an individual is stored in each individual's own memory as well as in the 'etheric' or universal mind regions of creation, so as to form a collective memory. In other words each action that a human makes is both a personal one and a collective one. In other words, it affects the individual and the universe simultaneously.

Personal memories or impressions each have amplitude. That is, they are mild, medium or strong, depending on the intensity of the action. These stored impressions contain information, just as a seed of a flower does. Each seed knows what it will become. An acorn has within it the information to become an oak tree, (given the right conditions).

Every impression will at some point manifest and will produce a circumstance that is suitable for its manifestation.

The Principle of Mind Fog.

This principle is called different things in different cultures. The Indians in the East call it <u>Maya or Illusion.</u> The Native Americans call it <u>Mitote or Fog.</u>

Illusion is the appearance of things as if they are real. When a magician pulls a rabbit out of the hat, it appears as if the rabbit was in the hat. When he pulls six rabbits out of the same hat, we are intrigued by his magic ability to create such an illusion. We inherently know that it is impossible for the hat to hold six rabbits, yet we see him do it and we cannot deny that there are six rabbits and a single hat.

We are caught in a state of illusion. But when the magician reveals to us how he does his trick, the magic disappears and the show is over. Once we know how the feat is performed, we are no longer trapped in the mind fog of illusion and we can grasp reality.

Life is a similar illusion. We mistake the real for the non real. We cling to the notion that what we see, hear, smell, touch and taste is real. We cling to our thoughts and perceptions, as the final arbiters of truth.

Because we lose the sense of who or what we really are, we develop a polarized view of life; we are attracted to some things and repelled by others. As a consequence, we like some things but despise others; we experience pleasure and pain and we cling to our own ego sense to try to help us find stability.

As a result of our ignorance of truth, we are afraid of death because we know that when we die, our ego will die too and our sense of who we think we are will then vanish.

35

The principle of Non Duality

There is a state of existence, beyond duality. If everything in creation (duality) is always changing then there must also be a state that is not created, which does not change, but which supports change and creation.

The state of non duality is a state that exists before duality arises. Because mind is a function of duality, as we will see later on, it is impossible for mind to grasp the non dual state. The non dual state exists before the mind is formed.

We thus need to constantly attach ourselves to the non dual state; that is, instead of holding on to a polarized viewpoint, we must stand aside from polarity and adopt the posture of a witness. This witness consciousness leads us to a state of non duality, an experience of true stability, no matter how high the waves in the stormy ocean of our lives.

The Principle of Free Will.

This is the principle that we have the power to make a choice. We can learn to take appropriate actions, which can overcome the trappings of Karma and which will lead us to move from a state of "Mind Fog" to a state of "Clarity".

It is only when we have cleared the trappings and lifted the fog that we can find ourselves in a state called abundance. The removal of the trappings and the lifting of the fog are the factors that facilitate our experience of the state of abundance, where the qualities of a true human lifestyle prevail, and where we can experience health, wealth, wisdom love and freedom.

The above four principles are the factors or the foundation principles of all practical life philosophies and religions. They are the direct working principles that have been handed down from master to disciple throughout the ages. Philosophies and religions have been built around them.

We will need to look at them in a little more detail, but a complete study of these principles can take a lifetime or even many lives to understand, and is not the purpose of this book. However, we do need to at least comprehend the basics regarding these four principles, if we want to be richly rewarded.

We need to study these principles from the perspective of a human being and through the mechanism of human functioning.

Mindset

At the outset, it is important to put the concept of mind into a perspective that we can relate to on an everyday basis. I am not talking about genius or some other "savant" quality. I am talking about patterns of behavior that can be instilled into our minds that will cause the attraction to those things and attributes that we want, but without creating a conflict internally.

An example of an internal conflict, for many people, is the belief that the pursuit of money is the very antithesis of a spiritual life. The desire for money has long been considered the root of all evil. A common question born out of this conflict is; how can we be spiritual human beings, yet be in pursuit of a "million dollars" so we can live a life of luxury? This presents for some, a real conflict. How is it possible to be in pursuit of spirituality and materiality at the same time?

Tantrics of India

The answer is derived from the teachings of the Tantrics of India, a Yoga sect whose philosophy and practices are amongst the most practical in the world. The Tantrics teach that our purpose, as humans, is to yoke together our body, mind and soul with that of the eternal reality in such a way that there is an experience of a divine consciousness, namely Self or God, **and to achieve this state by using the very qualities that we have been endowed with as humans.**

Tantra teaches that if one falls to the ground, then one must use the ground to stand up. In fact, every power that we are endowed with as humans, can and must be used for a divine purpose. This extends to our sexual energy as well as our material possessions. Sexual energy is the most fundamental energy and governs our instinct to procreate and extend the human race. We can use it or abuse it.

The more material resources we have, indicates that we have more opportunities to use them for spiritual purposes. Again we can use our monetary wealth or abuse it. This is true for any of our resources.

Nuclear power can provide light and heat to an entire nation or it can obliterate an entire nation. It is the intent or purpose to which we apply our resources that is important and potent. Without resources, whether personal energy, or money, or nuclear power, we are all mostly impotent.

Therefore, Tantra teaches that we can only really help others if we are first able to help ourselves. It is therefore, our prime responsibility to learn to help ourselves. This is not to be interpreted in a selfish way. The way in which we help ourselves is by helping others – by giving more than we take.

Mindset – a definition!

The American Heritage Dictionary offers the following two definitions;

- **A fixed mental attitude or disposition that predetermines a person's responses to and interpretations of situations.**

- **An inclination or a habit.**

From this definition we can deduce that *an attitude is a habit*. We can change our attitudes and therefore we can change our habits.

Habits are like little grooves that we make in a cold Jell-O with a hot knife. The more we think the same thoughts, the deeper become the grooves in our memory banks or mental structures. The arrangement of these grooves form patterns of behavior. The deeper the grooves, the more likely it is that our ideas, will follow these patterns. *The world that we perceive is a direct result of the patterns we have grooved into our minds.*

If we find that our world is not filled with abundance, we need to look at our habits. If every time we take an action, we keep getting the same results, it's probably because we are allowing our energy to flow along the same old patterns in our minds. Unfortunately, it takes an extra effort to change these patterns. The lazy way out is just to allow our energy to follow the same patterns over and over again.

To paraphrase Albert Einstein, who said; if we keep on doing what we have always done and expect different results each time, then we are probably insane. So if we do not find abundance, or rather, as we will see later, if abundance does not find us, then we need to check our personal habit patterns.

Part of the problem with the formation of habits is that sometimes they are formed out of ignorance. Most of us do what we <u>think</u> is right and will keep on doing the same thing over and over until we get the results we expect. We think that we just need to be persistent until we eventually succeed. And yet the more we keep at it, the deeper the grooves become and the more defined the pattern becomes and the less likely we are to achieve the results we anticipate. There is a disconnect between our wishes and our habit patterns.

However, it is altogether a different matter if we form habits that are not born out of ignorance. Habits that we inculcate with purpose and insight lead to patterns that **will** produce the exact response that we are anticipating. It is this very act of creating purposeful habits, that we call free will.

Habits perpetuate themselves. Habits by nature are

subconscious and cause us to behave automatically.

People tend to judge us by our actions rather than our words. For example, if we tell someone we will meet them at a certain time, but we arrive late, then people will know us by our actions and not our words. They will know that we are not punctual because we display non punctual behavior patterns.

Once we create purposeful actions, and repeat them until a purposeful habit is formed, we will then begin to see the magic. *The magic is that the universe responds to the habit pattern that we create.* If we create a loving habit then the universe will respond with all the loving that we can imagine. If we create a hateful habit, the universe will respond accordingly.

We are the creators of our own universe. We have to accept responsibility for our universe because we create it.

In the tradition of some Native Americans, they teach us that there are two wolves at war with each other, both of whom are living within each one of us. One is nasty and the other is kind and caring. Which wolf eventually wins the battle, is the one that we choose to feed!

So, if it is true abundance that we really want; abundance of love, of money, of recognition, of happiness, all we have to do is create or feed the right habit with the appropriate patterns.

What is wealth?

The American Heritage Dictionary defines wealth as;

- *An abundance or profusion of anything; a plentiful amount.*

There are only two reasons why we don't have abundance. Either our previous actions, or experiences, have created patterns that are preventing us from attracting abundance; or there is a disconnect between what we want (our wishes) and the kind of patterns we create, which are necessary to achieve our desires. That's it; only two reasons why we don't have what we want.

In fact *the only way to have abundance is through the power of attraction*. The power of attraction means becoming like a magnet and drawing it to us. We can only *attract* abundance. We cannot really get it any other way. If we try to force it, it will evaporate just as vigorously.

Abundance is like love. We cannot force someone to love us. We have to attract love. How do we attract it? Only by loving. Only by being in the state of loving, can we create that kind of energy that attracts other states of loving.

45

For every reaction that we encounter in our life, we probably only respond in one of three ways;

- We can fight!

- We can run!

- We can concede!

None of these is the way of abundance. The pure Zen of this is enormous.

If we fight we are creating a disharmony. If we run, we are not dealing with the issue at hand. If we give up, we are surrendering our purpose to that of someone else. This is why so many people cannot find abundance in their lives. They are hard wired to either fight, take flight or surrender.

So how on earth can we create abundance?

The answer is *by being in the state of abundance.* Once we enter into the state of abundance, we will have as much abundance as we want because abundance is all around us. If this sounds mystical, it probably is. However, it is true.

There is a saying in the teachings of the wise.

"Neither the lover nor the loved be – be but the loving!"

This is a fundamental principle, which we all should adhere to. It teaches us that as long as we are differentiating between subject and object, then the experience is missed. If I see myself as the lover and you as the beloved, I am caught in the description rather than the experience. The experience is the 'loving' – the energy flow between the lover and the beloved. The challenge is to identify with the experience and neither with the subject nor the object.

We also constantly miss the experience because we either dwell in the past or try to live in the future, instead of being alive in the present moment.

I ask with all the humility in the world. What good does it do us, to dwell in the past? What good does it do us to dream of the future?

You might challenge me by saying that we can learn from the past and that unless we learn from history, we are all doomed to repeat it. Or you might ask; what good is a life without a future? My answer is that there is a difference between being stuck in the past full of regrets about what we did or did not do or wishful or fanciful thinking about what might be in the future, instead of actually creating a future by being alive in the moment.

There is only one reality and that reality is now, in this very ever present moment.

It is only in the now that we can exercise our

will and control our thoughts and change our habits.

We cannot undo the past. We cannot blink into the future. If our present actions are not in accordance with our purpose, then our purpose will not manifest in the way we imagine.

There is no right and there is no wrong. There is just the inevitable result of our present moment actions.

Therefore, if it is 'abundance' that we want, which means having the ability to be in a state of abundance, then we have to change our habits and we have only the NOW in which to do it.

We cannot change our past and we cannot do anything in the future. There is only the NOW.

Because there is no judge and no jury, we only need to concern ourselves with the inevitable response to our own present moment thoughts and actions.

It is said that a wise person knows the future! What this saying really means is that a wise person knows the consequence of his or her actions.

But what do we humans really want?

If we analyze what people all over the world really want, we can categorize their wants and needs into five basic human desires:

1. HEALTH

2. WEALTH

3. WISDOM

4. LOVE

5. FREEDOM

These five desires are fundamental. We really need all five in order to experience the potential of fully developed human beings.

Let us look at each category.

Health: True health is when we human beings operate from a point of wholeness. When we are whole humans, we are centered, balanced and in a state of equanimity. Our bodies are functioning properly and naturally. Our bodies are flexible and pain free. Our minds are relaxed, creative and calm. Our breath is smooth and flows deeply with each inhalation and exhalation.

Wealth: True wealth is the ability to have choices in our lives. Choices can only come about when we have enough resources to do what we want, when we want. Wealth means having all that we need in order to operate as fully developed human beings. It does not mean having the largest yacht in the world.

There is a difference between the accumulation of money and having real wealth. What use is all the money in the world, if we are unhappy or constantly sick and can't even experience love in our lives.

Wisdom: Wisdom is the knowledge and the proper understanding of what it means to 'make a difference' in life. Wise people always make a difference. They leave a legacy. They provide something with which others can elevate themselves. Wise people are true leaders. Their wisdom enhances the lives of others. Wise people are creative, not competitive. They lead from behind by pushing others to the front.

Love: There is no life worth living without the power of love. Love is the quintessential force in our lives that gives everything a purpose. It is the power of synthesis. It is the power that pulls everything to the center. It is the power of attraction. One cannot force love. One can only attract love. In truth, it is the level of love in oneself that attracts love. Love attracts love. Love is the functional energy of the universe and is the power or force of life that sustains life. It is the quality that we call GOD. Love exists within us and without us.

Freedom: Freedom is the experience of non attachment. It is the ability to transcend the mental chatter and clutter and to exist as a witness consciousness. We are in the world, but we are not of it. We do not need to judge and we are not held hostage by opinions. We are in fact free from the tyranny of our own ego, that shadow quality that takes control of our lives and leads us into bondage. How can we have or exercise "Free Will" if we are not Free?

The five categories above, when taken as a group, are the categories that make up what may be called a "mindset." A truly satisfying and fulfilling lifestyle is one that is filled with health, wealth, wisdom, love and freedom. Each human being should try to integrate these five qualities into their lives and then to expand each one of them. When we have all five of these qualities, we are in a state of abundance.

Many people will cry out in despair and blame their circumstances for preventing one or more of these qualities from developing. Some people are given significantly greater opportunities than others. Can we compare the life of a child born into the home of a billionaire to that of a child born into the squalor of a refugee camp?

The answer is no. Not in a material sense. The circumstances are totally different. However, the child in the refugee camp may experience true love, compassion, family and community which may be denied to the billionaire child. Life experiences occur anywhere and everywhere. The real difference between these two circumstances is one of opportunity.

For those of us who are favored by opportunity, which comes to us through unconscious attraction, we need to be filled with gratitude. Each opportunity is a blessing, a realization of a seed of a previous effort that has now manifested into our life as a favorable circumstance. Because it is unconscious, we refer to it as 'luck', as if it arrived by random chance.

The acceptance of the law of cause and effect, as a basis for the workings of the universe is necessary and compelling, if we want to be able to create opportunities in the future. There is an intricate relationship between our Karma and our Free Will. We need to investigate this relationship and raise our consciousness to a level where we create positive Karma that will bring about a favorable response in the form of opportunity.

Free Will is the ability to choose, and thereby make the choices that initially create positive Karma. As we (humans) develop this ability, we become more and more perfected, ultimately reaching saintly levels where all our actions are no longer Karma producing.

Karma is a Sanskrit word meaning "action". All actions are binding in that they produce reactions. These reactions are always the effect of some action taken at some point in time.

If you want abundance but are skeptical, or even worse, if you are just plain cynical, you will need to suspend your cynicism and accept these beliefs for the time being.

Adopting these beliefs will help you to start a new mindset. Soon, you will be able to convert all your beliefs into knowing and this knowledge will be the result of direct experience. Direct experience is the only teacher that can change patterns in one's mind.

Our mindset is a function of three phases of deliberate action:

Step 1 (Preparation): Knowledge and deep acceptance of the four above principles that are necessary to prepare one's mind for the development of a mental framework that will lead to a state of abundance.

Step 2 (Terrain): Understanding the natural flow of energy. By tuning into this natural flow, we go with the tide not against it.

Step 3 (Appropriate Action): We must apply or implement certain ideas and practices that will be helpful in leading us to experience an abundant state.

The Human Factor

A Fivefold Entity

We as human beings can be understood, at a certain level, as a fivefold entity. We all have five senses (seeing, smelling, touching, tasting and hearing), and five sense organs (eyes, nose, skin, mouth, and ears). These senses are the equipment that each one of us has within a five-fold body matrix.

This matrix is described as follows, in accordance with its five different functions: Essentially, a human being is comprised of:

- A physical faculty - or food sheath

- An energy faculty - or breath sheath

- A mental faculty - or thought sheath

- An intelligence faculty – or discriminating sheath (power to choose)

- A wisdom faculty – or bliss sheath (ability to intelligently experience joy.)

Each sheath is interactively connected to each other sheath and thus forms an aura of energy, in different layers, around the physical body. This aura can be seen by clairvoyants and partially seen using Kirlian photography.

If we observe carefully, we will see that these five sheaths make up what is known as the "body-mind-soul " complex.

What we call our physical *body* is a combination of the *food and breath* sheaths.

What we call *mind* is the combination of *breath, thought and intelligence* sheaths.

What we call *soul* is the combination of the *intelligence and wisdom* sheaths.

Please note that the brain is a physical 'instrument' within the food sheath and is not the mind.

Physical Body

The physical body is called the food sheath because it depends on food and water for its existence. It absorbs food and water and extracts nutrients to sustain itself. Eventually when it is discarded at the point of death, the physical body naturally returns to the food chain, becoming food for other species.

Energy Body

The energy body is where the universal life force is gathered to supply the body with the energy to activate the organs and physical senses and to produce the breath. When breathing stops the body stops because the activating fuel or energy (life force) is no longer available to the body.

The entire nervous system is activated through the mechanism of the energy body or life force sheath. In martial arts, it is this life-force energy, called Ki or Chi or Prana that is used to create so much power.

Mental Body

The mental body, or thought sheath, is where all the impulses from the physical senses are recorded. On the one hand the mental body takes in sensory data from the physical body, via the energy body, and on the other hand it has access to wisdom and discrimination, namely the power to choose, from the intelligence and wisdom sheaths.

Therefore, the mental body acts as a bridge between the inner dimensions and the outer dimensions. Because the mental body is a bridge with one side connected inwards to the soul and the other side connected outwards to the body, the human experience is that of duality.

Inner and Outer Dimension

We all have a constant experience of both an inner and an outer dimension. The mental body uses the entire nervous system, brain and spinal cord to convert thoughts into feelings and actions. Everything that is created changes, therefore, there is nothing that we can perceive with our five senses (smell, touch, hearing, taste, sight) that is permanent.

Since nothing is permanent, then even conditions like suffering, poverty, illness or pain are also not permanent and ultimately will pass or can be willfully changed. This is also true of all the pleasures in life, which are also not permanent. It is a fact that in the case of the accumulation of possessions, that either the possessions will ultimately be removed from the person or the person will ultimately be removed from the possessions. One of these two conditions is inevitable.

Intelligence

We can describe the fivefold nature of man by dividing intelligence into five parts.

- Experience of Instincts or Cravings

- Experience of Moral Code – Good vs Evil

- Experience of Abstract or Intellectual Concepts

- Experience of a Creative Force

- Experience of Divine Unity

Each of these stages represents phases of evolutionary growth. Mankind is evolving from the instinctual levels of energy or consciousness toward the experience of unity or a state of non duality.

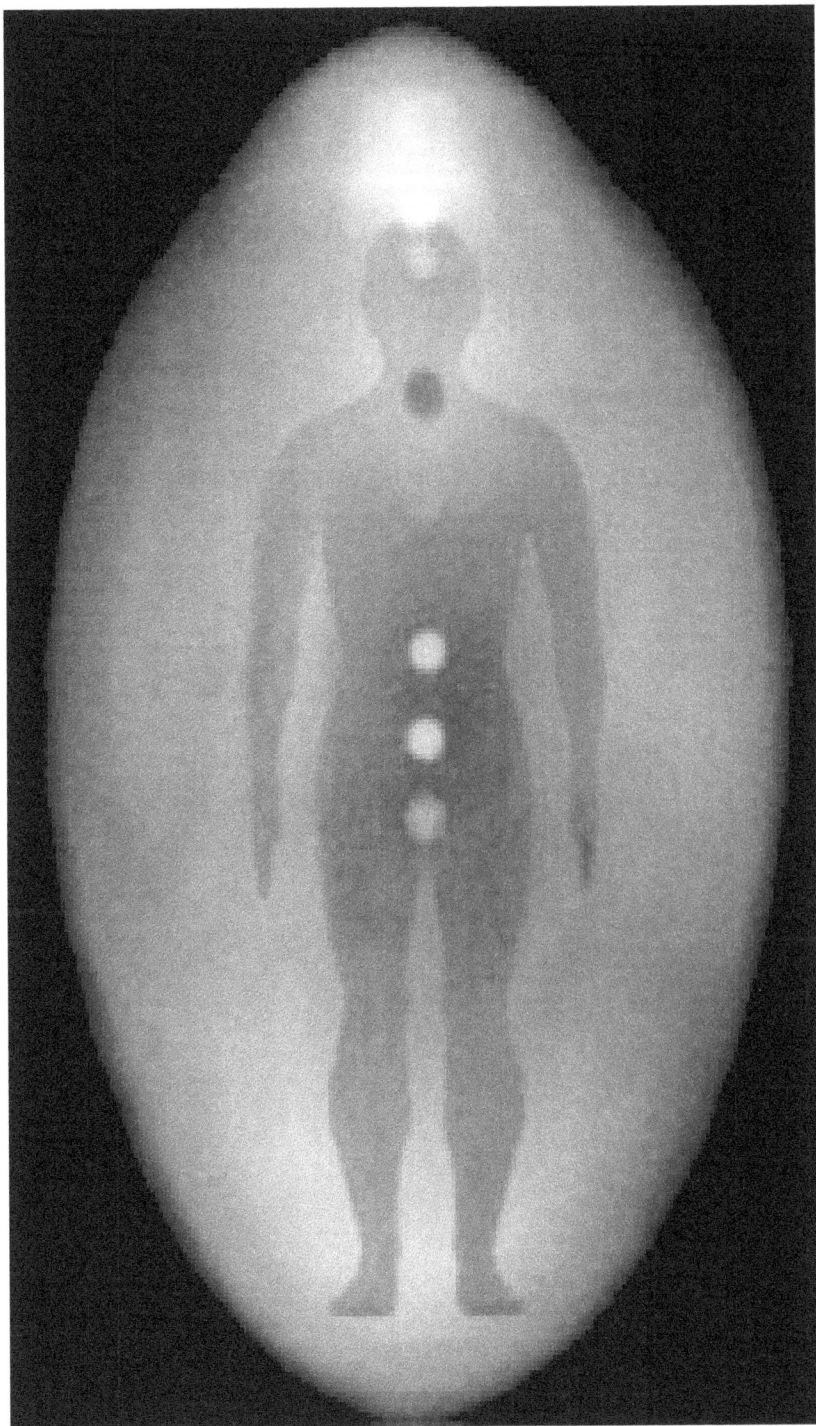

This is how creation proceeds and is the direction in which all creation is headed.

By learning how to properly use the "bridge" faculty or mind, we can bring about the experience of abundance or fulfillment into our lives. Our world is derived from the actions of mind and it is this ability that leads to success or if you prefer, greater evolutionary development.

Having some notion of our fivefold structure, we are now ready to examine the four principles in greater detail.

Karma
The Law of Cause and Effect:

"Sow a thought, reap an act
Sow an act, reap a habit
Sow a habit, reap a character
Sow a character, reap a destiny"

This amazingly profound proverb characterizes the principle of Karma in a nutshell.

The issue that we as humans face is that when we were born into this physical life, we each arrived with our own individual Karmic record. We did not arrive with a clean state. We arrived with some baggage. In our arrival package, we each contain a record of all the impressions that we have ever experienced as a result of our previous thoughts or actions. Accordingly, because of our different Karmic records, we are **not** all born equal.

Each impression that we carry in our record, is like a seed that must either manifest (grow) at some point in time or which must be 'cooked' before it grows. "Cooking the seeds" is an important way to enhance our spiritual growth. How well we cook these latent seeds will determine how much progress we make spiritually.

If the seeds are not cooked they will manifest; some of them in this life, and either in a mild, moderate or extreme way. *The combination of our seeds manifesting, and our reactions to the experiences they produce, is what we experience as our world.* Some seeds produce suffering and others produce joy.

These seeds form the patterns of our behavioral tendencies. Some tendencies can be modified while other tendencies cannot.

For example, one person may be born into a very pale, light skinned, sensitive body while another person may be born into a darker, more pigmented body. The person with the light skin may be predisposed to skin cancer from too much exposure to the sun while the darker skinned person may enjoy hours in the sun with little negative effect. Science calls these Karmic seeds, genetic predispositions.

As a result of these particular seeds, the light skinned person is more likely to be an indoor type and may turn to more cerebral activities throughout his or her life. On the other hand, the darker skinned person, who can tolerate the sun, may become more outgoing and athletic.

WE ARE THEREFORE, PREDISPOSED TO OUR DESTINIES BECAUSE OF OUR TENDENCIES, WHICH WERE CREATED BY US DURING PREVIOUS EXPERIENCES, AND AS

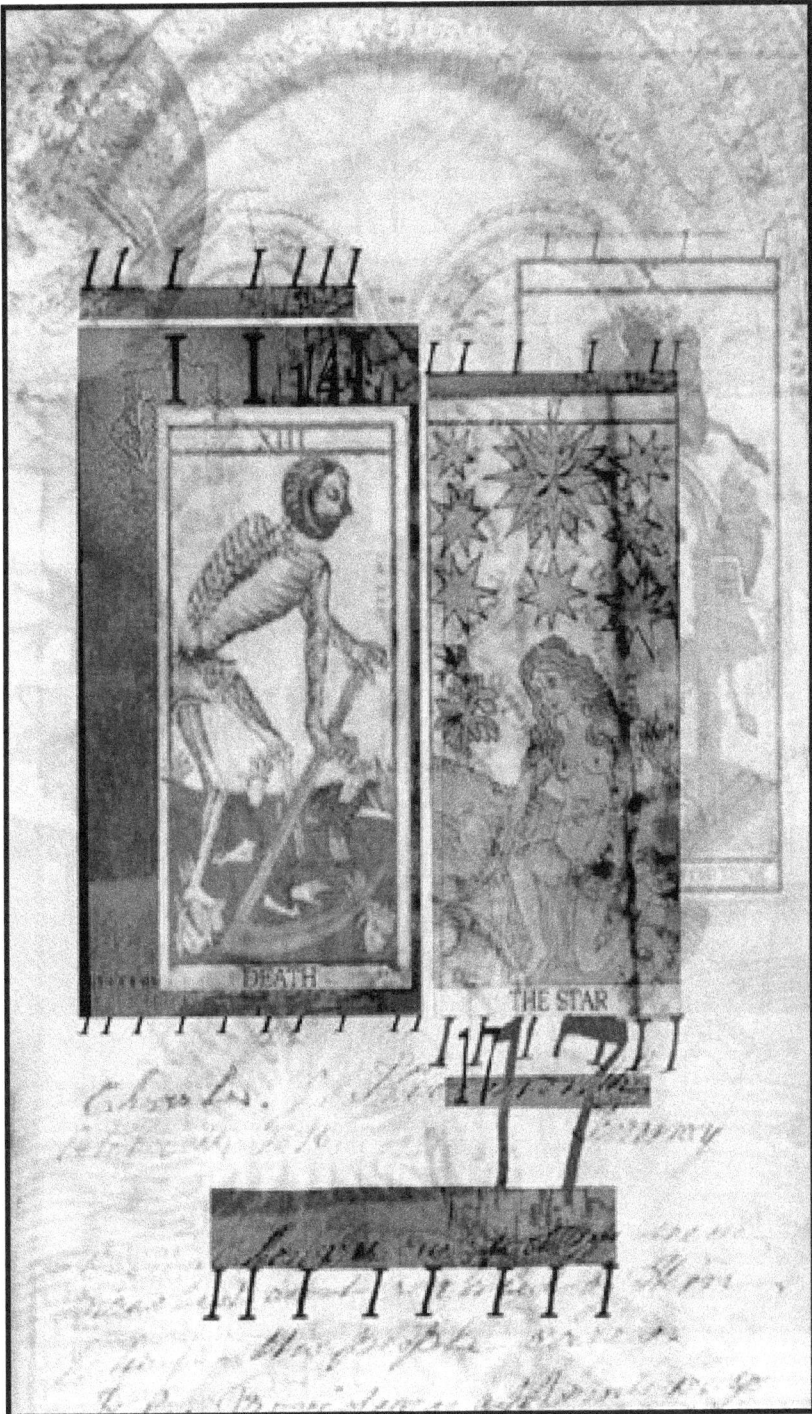

CONSEQUENCES OF OUR PREVIOUS THOUGHTS AND
ACTIONS.

There are five kinds of Karma. For practical purposes, they are;

Total Karma – the sum total of all our experiences ever recorded in our memory banks, and which are stored as latent impressions.

Ripe Karma – those latent impressions, which are now manifesting in this life.

Changeable Karma - those impressions which are not yet ready to manifest.

Group Karma - common experiences among groups of people who have been formed into groups because their collective mind has the need for similar experiences.

Future Karma - those impressions that have not yet been recorded and are dependent on our present actions and thoughts in order to take form.

Total Karma is the sum total of all impressions ever received by an individual soul in the journey throughout life. Whether one believes in reincarnation or not, *the reality is that every individual has to face the circumstances of his or her own making.* This is the basis of taking responsibility for oneself.

If we accept that we are in a position or circumstance of our own making then, we can make the necessary changes to improve our future. Whereas, if we believe the fault and responsibility lies somewhere else, then there can be no possible way for us to make any corrections for ourselves, and thus our own destiny is in someone else's hands.

However, this is not the case, since *we caused the patterns to form, we also have the opportunity to correct any fault causing patterns*. This fact provides real hope.

We cannot escape our "Ripe" Karma, those tendencies that are due to manifest in this life time and which produce the events and circumstances that we must experience. *What we can change though is how we experience these circumstances.*

Certain experiences will be joyful and others sorrowful. By responding in a proper way to the events and circumstances that we experience, we have the opportunity to learn new ways to behave and think so that we do not reproduce or repeat negative patterns.

We can also learn to 'cook' the seeds. By 'cooking' the latent seeds that are within us, we can modify the negative Karma that we previously created and bring about a modified experience of our Karma. But Karma is the law of action and reaction, and therefore what we sow, so shall we reap.

The best way to approach Karma is by first learning to *resist the urge to react*. Reaction is often the cause of binding Karma, because we do not stop to think. When we stop to think, we learn to allow the energy of the circumstance to diffuse.

In emergency situations it is necessary sometimes to respond quickly and positively in order to avert a catastrophe. However, there is a difference between responding and reacting. Usually when one is responding to an emergency situation there is no thought of I, but rather just a natural response of preparedness that is not ego based. The fact that the ego is not involved is what makes the difference.

Karma is the way the universe works. Karma or action is what every human being does every moment of the day. There is really no such thing as inaction. Even sitting in a cave and meditating is action.

Karma can work for us or work against us; it depends on whether our actions are 'ego' based or 'other' based. 'Other' always implies service or sacrifice.

There is salvation from crippling Karma and it is this; we always have the opportunity to change our attitude and create good quality habits.

There is no God judging what we do as good or bad.

The Universe is a self correcting mechanism and is also self policing in that regard. Justice is always served. We serve justice to ourselves at some point in time. The wheels of the gods grind slowly, but they grind exceedingly fine! So what goes around, comes around.

By examining our tendencies yet ***not reacting*** to our impulses, we diminish their tyranny and thereby provide ourselves with the opportunity to create different kinds of experiences. We have the ability to therefore effectively change ourselves. We are solely in control of our "changeable" Karma by refusing to react to negative impulses.

For example, if we encounter a smelly homeless person on the side of the road, do we feel disgust, which is easy to feel, or do we feel compassion? Compassion is the high road and will create non toxic Karma from which we alone will benefit. Further, if we are kind to the homeless person, he will be uplifted by our kindness and amazingly, so will we.

"Group" Karma is the tendency that has accrued to a group of similar minded people, who have come together because of *common patterns in the collective unconscious regions of the mind.* Therefore events happen in groups as a result of common identification with the tendencies within the 'group mind'.

The question of why do bad things happen to good people often comes up in reference to events that involve groups. There will always be a debate about the injustice of the calamities that happen to so called good people, through seemingly no fault of their own.

A deeper reflection can show us that it may not really be the way it all seems. For example, a car full of young children dying in an accident at an early age, seems like a tragedy of insurmountable proportion to most people and especially to the parents or other loved ones. But from a point of view of a higher consciousness, the children may very well have had a short earth life, just long enough for them to clear previously created Karma, so that they can be ready for the experience of a very long "heavenly" or astral life. Death is only a physical body change.

"Future" Karma is the Karma that will result from the actions that we are taking now and will manifest at some future point in time. This is the easiest Karma to consider because it is not yet set in any fixed vibratory pattern. Therefore, we have the opportunity to make our bed, so that we can comfortably lie in it.

Karma is really one of the foundations of a Universal Truth. It is the mechanism of a universal justice system without the need for any outside judge or jury. In the final analysis, we are all our own judges.

Our actions create our lives and ultimate destinies, so it is not a question of whether Karma is or is not true, but rather how best we should think and behave, if we intend to create a joyful state of abundance or clarity.

An archer is a useful metaphor to understand Karma. Arrows are equivalent to our Karmic tendencies. The bow is equivalent to our mind. Those arrows that have been fired by our bow and are in the air are the "ripe" Karmas. They are already in play and will either produce experiences that make us happy or which will cause suffering. Therefore, our life experiences are symbolized by the flying arrows.

The arrows in the quiver have yet to be fired. The quiver may contain either poison arrows or love arrows or a combination of both. The poison arrows, when they are fired, will be experienced by us as suffering, whereas the experiences produced by love arrows will be experienced as joy.

By changing our attitudes, and therefore our habit patterns, we can start to store more and more love arrows into our quivers.

Understanding and working to negate negative Karma becomes the starting point of a purposeful and successful life. The question then is what to do about past Karma. How can we fix what has led to negative "blockers?" There are two solutions and both need to be undertaken simultaneously.

- *The first is to start creating "good" Karma; we can change our habits by changing our attitude and thoughts. We can start to add "positive" arrows to our quiver.*

- *The second is to "cook the seeds" by changing our consciousness through meditation. We will discuss meditation in a later chapter.*

In order to start seeing positive results in our life we need to pay attention to our thoughts and actions. By becoming a purposeful human being and contributing to the world with intensity and passion, our lives will absolutely change by a hundred and eighty degrees. Redefining our attitudes from selfish to unselfish is a key step in achieving this change.

Contrary to popular belief, it is not the rewards of our actions that we must care about, but rather the process. In fact, we need to surrender all concerns about the results and pay full attention to the process of our thoughts and actions. The rewards will take care of themselves. *It is the appropriate effort that is important and not the reward.*

For example, if we are in business trying to sell something to our potential customer, and if we are only worried about the money that we can obtain from the customer, instead of the service we can provide, then our focus is on the wrong pattern for producing the Karma that will lead to abundance.

To negate negative patterns, consider the following story. (This story indicates how we can take appropriate action to weaken the effects of negative Karma).

During the rule of Mahatma Gandhi in India, there was a particularly fierce clash one day between a group of Hindus and a group of Muslims. During the clash, a Hindu child was killed. The father of the deceased child, filled with anger and the thoughts of revenge, tracked down a Muslim family, and in a moment of hate, killed a Muslim child. After realizing what he had done, and filled with pain and guilt, he approached the Mahatma and related the story to him.

In Hindu tradition, the instructions of the Guru are very important, so he asked the Mahatma what he should do in order to overcome the incredibly negative Karma he had just created. The Mahatma advised him as follows;

"Go find a Muslim family, one in which the parents have been killed, thus causing a child to be orphaned, then take that child and raise it as your own - but make sure you raise the child as a Muslim"

In this example, two actions were needed to be taken; first the taking in and raising of an orphaned child. Second, the raising of the child as a Muslim, since that is the faith into which the child was born. The greatness of this story is in the wisdom of a clear action necessary to change attitudes and habits.

In order to know whether the Karma we create is binding or not, we need to determine if the actions we take are leading us towards unity or away from unity. Actions that lead us and others toward unity are productive of non binding and helpful Karmic patterns.

Mind Fog - Maya or Mitote

The way we know life is by what is reflected to us from the apparent world outside of ourselves. In fact, whatever we see, hear, smell, touch or taste is the result of energy that is reflected from the outside world into one or more of our sense organs and then transmitted by the nervous system to our brain where it is processed. Once these energy impulses are processed, the impressions are then compared with data in our storage banks (memory). Based upon our previous learning, they are then given meaning.

Let us take an example. Suppose, we are walking in the forest and we come upon a snake ahead of us, lying on our pathway. We immediately stop because the image of the snake is reflected to our eyes, then to our brain and compared in our data banks to other data, and finally ranked according to any previous notion of what we may have of a snake.

According to that notion, is how we will respond! If we are very used to handling snakes and are not afraid, we may go about our walk and simply persuade the snake to move off the path, or allow it to do so of its own accord.

On the other hand, if we are terrified of snakes, through inexperience or ignorance, we may turn and run the other way. Or we may try to kill the snake so as to remove the fear from within us.

In reality, the total experience occurs within us. If the emotion of fear is generated, we will behave one way, and if the emotion of acceptance is generated, we will behave in a totally different way.

The snake on the path is never seen for what it is, but rather as a perception, after being filtered through our human response mechanisms.

In fact, nothing in the outside world is ever seen for what it is, but always through our filters of perception.

It is said that the outside world exists for the benefit of every human being; to bring about the experience of Self consciousness.

When we meet a person in our life whom we love, that person exists for the purpose of our experiencing love. If we meet someone we hate, then that person exists, for our benefit, to teach us about the qualities of hate. Neither the hate nor the love is in the other person. Both qualities are experienced within us, but are amplified or brought to a conscious state by the reflection from the other "person".

These vastly important experiences are meant to awaken the "witness" within us. The witness is the Self that is the unchanging unit of life, which in reality is who we are.

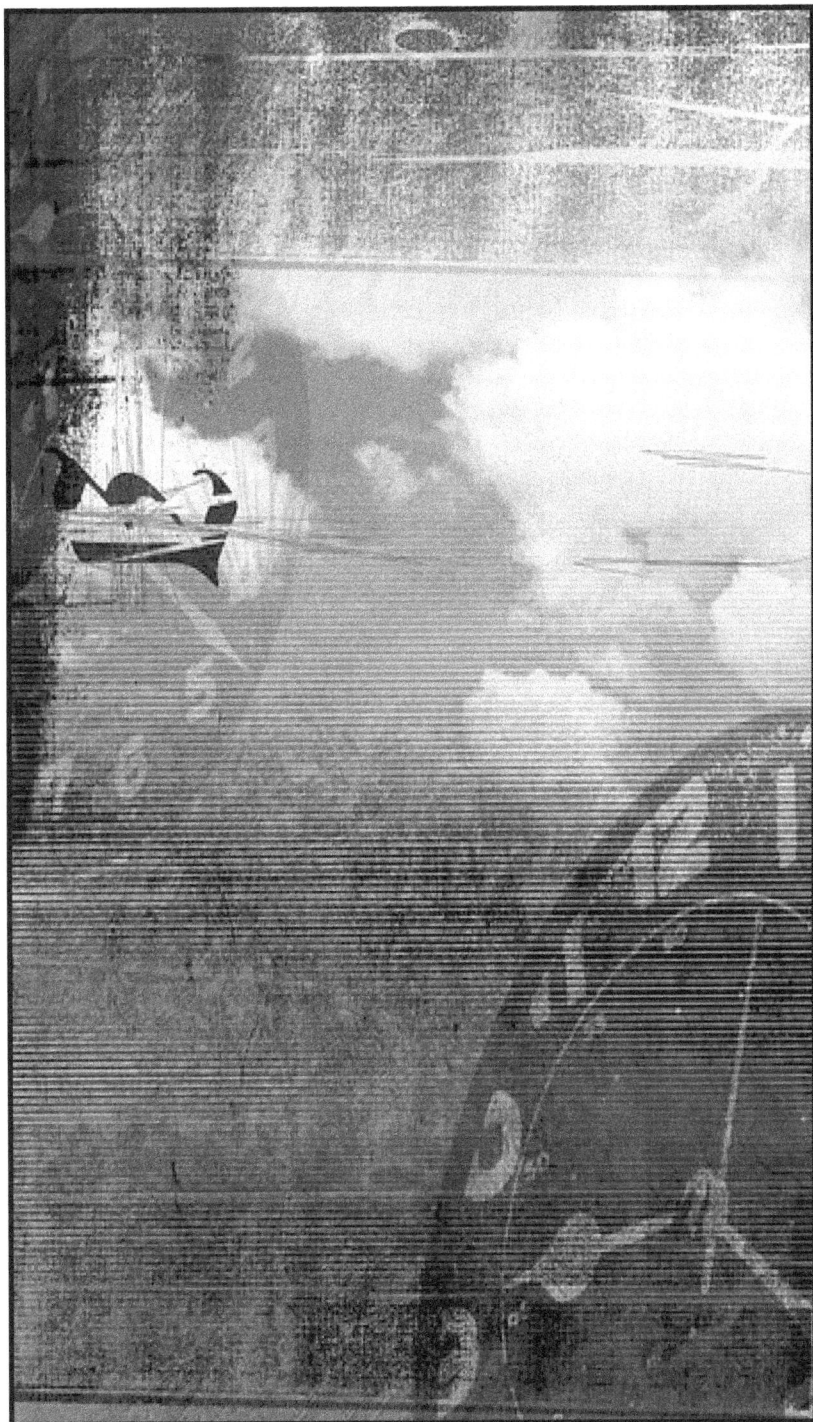

It is a very childish response to blame any outside situation or person for what we experience. The outside energy is there to amplify and awaken the experience within us so that we can grow from the energy transfer.

All of creation therefore,exists for our benefit. How we respond to our outside world is in accordance with the level of our maturity as humans.

Until we realize that the experience of the universe as being outside of us, and that all our sense organs and consequent sensory experiences are actually within us, we are in a state of Mind Fog. We are lost in an illusion, which we wrongly identify as truth.

However, the experiences are real and they occur for our benefit so that we can evolve to higher orders of being. We all need to grow, physically, mentally and spiritually.

Certain experiences will force us to grow and are thrust upon us. For example, we return home one day only to be confronted by a burglar who is in the process of plundering our home? How do we engage such a lesson and benefit from it?

Here we return to the issue of Karmic patterns. Since it is we who have created those seeds of energy at some time in the past, we are now experiencing a ripening of such a seed. The experience, therefore, can be mild, medium or intense. This is in proportion to the Karmic tendency that is ripening.

Perhaps the vibration we transmit when we confront the burglar is not one of fear, but rather tolerance. If our positive tendencies (vibrations) are strong enough to overcome the negative tendencies (vibrations) of the burglar, a certain magic takes place and the threat of being attacked by the burglar is negated.

Recently it was reported on the news, (this is a true story), that a burgler had entered the home of a group of people who were sitting on their patio eating and drinking some cheese and wine. The burglar, who was hooded, held a gun to their fourteen year old girl's neck and demanded money from the group. One adult said to the burglar, "your mother would be ashamed of you"! Whereupon the burglar responded that his mother was deceased, and immediately fell into a morose state.

Another adult in the group then offered the burglar some wine, which he gratefully accepted. After drinking the wine, he confessed that he had come to the wrong place and immediatley departed, having neither harmed anyone nor stolen from them.

In the converse, if our vibrations are not of the quality of love, and we therefore respond with anger or fear, our chance of confrontation with the burglar is much greater. The quality of our tendencies is not a mental thing but rather spiritual. Our vibrations, and not our thoughts, are what will have a direct influence on the burglar.

Never forget that our vibrations don't lie. People can feel intuitively what we are all about. We cannot really deceive people by thinking thoughts of deception. The energy bodies of other people are sensitive to vibrations of energy and can immediately determine our energy patterns and decide consciously or subconsciously whether they are comfortable or not.

I once witnessed a person being approached by a wild lion and then being licked by the ferocious looking lion, rather than being savaged. I can assure you that it had nothing to do with what the person was thinking or saying, but rather with the quality of the vibrations of the person, which the lion perceived as loving and non threatening.

The concept of Mind Fog is thus very important when building an "attractive mindset". Most motivational information is based on positive "thinking". While "positive" thoughts are better than "negative" thoughts, they do not have the same power as "positive vibrations" which are the result of true changes in the level of one's consciousness. Truth is a quality of soul and not of mind. The mind by itself is incapable of directly cognizing truth.

Non Duality

This principle may be the hardest of all to grasp. In fact, it is impossible to grasp with the mind. Remember, we discussed previously that the mind is a dual instrument; it externalizes and it internalizes. Thus it is only capable of perceiving a constant dual state. In order to grasp the state of non duality, we need to turn on our intuitive faculties, which is to say, a spontaneous grasping of that which is beyond the reach of the conscious mind.

The gradual grasping of Truth is an intuitive response that only arises after certain progress has been made in the evolution of consciousness. Until we have evolved to such a level of consciousness, all we can do in the meantime, is to try and use language and metaphor to point the way to the experience. The total experience of Truth is like no other experience in life. It is outside of the realm of perception and therefore is beyond all thought.

One way to try to apprehend the experience is through meditation. Meditation, in this sense is the quieting of all the incessant activities of the mind. These activities are provoked by the combination of sensory input, i.e. what we see, hear, smell, touch and taste. They are also provoked by what information is stored in the subconscious memories of the mind.

The first step towards reaching the level of stillness necessary for the experience of Truth is to learn to switch off the senses, one by one, so that they are no longer a stimulus. This requires practice and more practice.

One Ancient Wisdom suggests focusing all our energy on our breathing. The more we focus on our breath, the more it will slow down until eventually it becomes imperceptible. The more our breath slows, the quieter will our minds become. Another Ancient Wisdom suggests focusing on our heart beat. The more we focus on the pulse beat of our heart, the slower the heart will beat and eventually it will also become almost imperceptible. Again there is a link between breath and mind because, as we concentrate on our heartbeat, our breath stills, which in turn leads the mind to stillness. This focus, or attention on one point, results in the termination of any sensory input. There will be no more stirring up of the mental waves.

However, once the senses are turned off, our subconscious memories become very active because the mind, which needs fuel from the senses in order to operate, now has to find a different stimulus. So once there are no senses providing the stimuli, it turns to the energy stored in the individual's memory bank.

A lot of suppressed material will often surface that will cause anguish to the person meditating. At this point it is important to learn to be a "witness" and to be able to watch the movie in our mind, without being in any way emotionally attached.

It is also at this point that we have the opportunity to retrain or reset the subconscious pattern so that the experience that we are re-witnessing, feels positive. Once we negate a negative experience by inducing a positive one in its place, we reprogram our subconscious memories. The mind cannot tell whether an experience is actual or induced and will thus respond to the new program.

Again, practice makes perfect. These uprising impressions from the memory are Karmic tendencies. By allowing them to surface they will often evaporate – just as a bubble of air rising in a glass of water evaporates when it reaches the surface.

This process is also one of the best methods I know for curing neuroses. When a habit is so ingrained that it governs our free will, then that is a neurosis. Constant meditation, as I have just described, will help to eliminate the tendency. This is what is called "cooking the seeds".

Finally, once the mind come to rest because there are no sensory inputs coming from the physical senses or any thoughts rushing up from the sub conscious, then at that point there is no longer a need for a perceptive faculty, and the ocean of mind as it were, becomes calm enough to see through to the bottom; this "seeing through the ocean" offers us our first glimpse of Truth (Non Duality).

It is said that when a person can abide in this clarity, then all the Karma and the Illusion (Fog) is dispelled and a person is filled with an abundance of bliss, knowledge, and the experience of Truth. Then it is possible to attain all that one desires.

The principle of Appropriate Action

We need to constantly take the appropriate actions that will clear Karma and Mind Fog and bring ourselves to the state of Abundance or the 'REAL' mindset.

Illusion

We create illusion through ignorance. Let me give you some examples of mind fog or illusion. We know, or at least we should know, that the earth is spinning on its axis every day. In each 24 hours the earth will make a complete rotation of 360 degrees. We also know that each year the earth will revolve around the sun. In fact the earth is hurtling through space at a rate of about 67,000 miles per hour. The earth is in constant, rapid movement *yet we perceive that we are standing still* and we walk around oblivious to the fact that we are passengers on the earth-ship traveling at some amazingly fast speed.

In another example, we can only see what we call the visible portion of the electromagnetic spectrum, from red light through to violet light. We don't see radio waves or gamma waves or x-rays and so on, yet they are there. Hawks can see things from a mile away that humans can't. Therefore, what we see may not be the whole story.

It is very important then, as we develop a "mastery of mind consciousness," that we understand that what we perceive is **not** the truth; that the world "out there" is a reflection of the world "in here" and that we are completely responsible for how we experience both our inner and our outer worlds.

We need to learn to take the appropriate actions that will clear the Fog and wipe the slate of negative Karma so that we can reveal the state of Abundance.

Before we start on the 10 stages of progress or Gifts, as I like to call them, it is important to reiterate that Truth alone is real. By real, I mean permanent. Everything else is changing.

As long as something changes, it is technically not real. If it is changing how can it be real? The state before the change is different to the state after the change, therefore, which state is the real one? Is the caterpillar real or is the butterfly real? Many will argue that both are real. But, in truth both forms are transient, both forms are born and both forms die. However, the spark of life in both forms is real and does not die. Therefore, the spark of life is true and definitely real, whereas the outer forms are transient and changing.

Perceptions.

As humans, we constantly create our own sense of reality or truth *based on our perceptions.* What we perceive, we proclaim as truth and reality. What we proclaim, however, is based on ego and ego is our sense of separateness from everything else. This sense of separateness is, in fact, a part of the Mind Fog. The simple truth is that we are not separate entities but only appear to be because of the Illusion or Mind Fog, which causes us to confuse the real with the unreal.

So is our world, with all its contents and problems real? Yes, to our ego sense it is all real. Our world and all its perceived problems *are* real but only from the perspective of the participating ego. To us as individual egos, we ascribe reality to the transient and call the true reality an illusion. We have it exactly backwards. In order to reverse this key error, we need to let go of the sense of ego.

But eliminating the ego cannot be done with the mind, since the mind is a part of the ego. As we grow spiritually, we start to experience tastes of Truth, more and more, and in that experience the ego starts to diminish. Becoming absorbed in the state of Truth means the automatic and total annihilation of the sense called ego. In fact, ego collapses like a phantom when it encounters the Truth. Remember the biblical expression "No one can see My face and live".

When we are doing something that we are truly passionate about, there is no sense of time and there is no sense of "I am doing something that I am passionate about." There is just the experience of doing. No ego is involved.

Take a walk in the desert. One of the amazing experiences is the appearance of a mirage; an oasis where none really exists. We are so thirsty and parched that we will walk persistently towards the mirage in the hope of finding water. When we reach the mirage, it disappears like a phantom. This is what the ego does when we arrive at the Truth.

The aphorism of Plato – "Know thyself" should be stressed here as "Know thy Self".

Just as fish swimming in the ocean have no idea of water, so we as humans walk around each day breathing, but remain unaware of the air that we breathe. We do not see the air we breathe and seldom, if ever, do we think about it, unless it stops being there. This is mind fog or ignorance.

This ignorance leads to likes and dislikes, which in turn leads to pain and pleasure, which in turn culminates in our fear of death or the remaining in the fog because we cling to ego. This ignorance is the cause of all our suffering. In this fog we cannot see who we really are, so we make believe we are the ego.

In the next section we will examine the 10 stages of progress that will help us to realize how energy unfolds. This awareness provides us with a natural harmonious way to develop and arrive at a state of abundance.

As we become more and more adept at using these gifts every day, we will find that we become less and less bound to the Fog and more and more amenable to experiencing the Truth by living our lives more and more purposefully and in harmony with the Natural.

Ten Stages To Master Mind

Part 2 . The Terrain

What follows now is an outline of the 10 stages of creative progress, into which we can tune our mind and which will enable us to make our lives more productive. These natural evolutionary streams of energy are the "gifts" or the tools we have available to us in our 'mindset creating toolbox'.

By consciously harmonizing with the process that each of these powers represent, we will be better able to utilize the natural energy system of the universe to improve the way we understand and do things. The universe itself develops along the lines or patterns outlined in these 10 power expressions.

These power stages are symbolized by the numbers 1 through 9 plus the symbol 0.

Symbols are important constructs, as they reach back further into the human soul than what language can do. Language as a spoken word creates perceptions based on interpretations and implied meanings of the language.

Symbols however, communicate visually in the same way that music communicates aurally. Sound and Form are two tools that can be used to change consciousness when used in a scientific way.

In India, certain highly evolved Yogis make use of the science of Mantra and Yantra. Mantra is a sound, a root sound, that when chanted either aloud or inwardly, causes sound vibrations to impinge on the human psyche and bring about certain effects.

Yantra is a shape or form, derived from number, that does the same thing. The combination of sound and shape becomes a powerful tool in the hands of those who know this sacred science. Its purpose is to remove the Fog and to clear Karmic tendencies by changing the structure and wave formations in the mind.

With that in mind, let us then look at the ten power stages that creation unfolds as it **G**enerates–**O**perates-**D**issipates. We can learn to apply the process to our own creative skills.

By the way, *creation is a projection out of a state of non manifested consciousness.* As creation unfolds it reflects aspects of that creative consciousness. Eventually all creation will be withdrawn back into a non manifested state. Put another way, creation is a projection by a super conscious force onto a screen of matter. This pure unchanging projecting force is symbolized by the number 0.

Each one of us as part of this force, has this power

to create, albeit at a greatly reduced amplitude. We have the power to project our own creation. As above–so below.

Since we, as humans, are endowed with the creative mind force it is the reason why we have the power and ability to create. By flowing with the manifested 9 power principles and phases, we can develop our abilities in the most natural way.

Stage 1: Synchronicity.

Synchronicity is the power of the universe as it operates as a "simultaneously interconnected whole". Everything is a part of everything else. Universe comes from Latin and means "one song". Indeed, we are all notes in this one song. We use the number 1 as a symbol for synchronicity. Synchronicity is the power of "simultaneous connectedness". Psychologists use the term to describe a "meaningful coincidence".

The world appears like a hologram. In other words, the part appears in the whole and the whole is in every part. So when one part of the system is affected the entire system is simultaneously affected. As in a spider's web when the fly touches just one strand of the web, the entire web is alerted to its touch.

By focusing our attention on any one single aspect or point within the universe, our consciousness expands to bring into focus all the related elements connected to that point of focus.

How this plays out in everyday life is as follows. Suppose we become interested in buying a blue Honda motor car. Then as we bring the Honda car more and more into our field of awareness, we start to notice more and more Honda cars on the road. In fact we even start to notice how many Hondas are blue. Perhaps we might even pick up a magazine and on the cover see a feature picture of a blue Honda car. This is the universe responding to our focus because, as we focus consciousness, we activate energy. As we energize something, we get a response.

As individuals we can focus consciousness like a flashlight in the dark. We can shine it on any imagined object or cause. This brings that object or cause, more and more into our reality. Since our focus is on a Honda, the car will magically start to appear for us in different ways.

By focusing and visualizing, we will have expanded our consciousness to create what our thoughts are thinking. Try this for yourself. Pick something on which to focus. It requires proper visualization and focus. Practice it for a while and see what happens! If you want something for yourself, learn how to visualize it in fine detail and to desire it with total intensity. The universe will cooperate to provide it.

Be careful though what you wish for – you may just get it!

So understanding the power of synchronicity becomes a gift, if we use it consciously. It is triggered by what we focus on as a singular point of interest; the universe then cooperates to bring this point into focus for us.

Stage 2: Cooperation.

Everything in nature cooperates. That means everything operates together – cooperates. Nature does not see life as a duality or a series of oppositions, such as I am right and therefore you are wrong, but rather as a necessary *complementary antagonism*. In a battery, both poles are required in order to generate the flow of current.

Everything in the universe is there for our benefit. How is everything there for our benefit? By being a test for us. The test is to learn how to cooperate. Everything that happens to us, and every person that we meet, and every experience that we have is in some way a test of cooperation.

When we meet someone who shoots negative vibrations at us by being mean or nasty in some way, how do we react? If we react in a way that is just as nasty or negative, which is our choice, since we have free will, then we have been pulled down to the level of the nasty energy that we experienced. It is better to remain silent and to practice love so that we don't absorb toxic energy and harbor it within us.

Therefore, the gift of cooperation is to bring opposites into our life, so we can learn to harmonize with them. Some of the best relationships we can have are with people who appear to be opposite to us. Opposites attract. Therefore the gift of Cooperation provides us with the opportunity to find the complimentary antagonism and incorporate its power into our being, rather than waste our own power by fighting it.

Within a synchronous world, all parts cooperate. All atoms include positive protons that have a significant but polarized relationship with the negative electrons spinning around their nuclei. The cooperation of the proton and the electron causes the creation of all kinds of elements.

By taking the opposite point of view, instead of seeing it as an antagonism, we can learn to see it as a complement. Cooperating with the opposite point of view to that of our own, often leads to a more synergistic solution.

Stage 3: Creative Expression.

The universe actually renews itself through the creative expression in which two parts cooperate to create a third. This third force is the basis of all impulses coming into one's being as ideas. The polarity of the two cooperative energies leads to the expression of a third. A male and a female must cooperate in order to make a child.

All our creative endeavors result from our impulse to change something. For example, if you have a certain skill and I, have a problem, and *if* you are creative, you then have the opportunity to apply your skills to solve my problem.

This is why we need to understand the power of cooperation. In this case, we are opposites in the sense that I have a problem and you don't and in addition you have a skill that I don't. Therefore, we are opposites because we have opposing conditions. However, we complement each other because I have something for you, namely a problem to fix, and you have something for me, namely a solution. Therefore by cooperating we create a wonderful synergy. We should seek this synergy whenever we encounter an opposite.

The opportunity to cooperate is all around us. In business we might call this a "joint venture". In a friendship, we would call it a "relationship". There are an unlimited number of ways that we can find to cooperate with others around us that will lead to a strong synergy. Our creative cooperation can be materialized further as it enters the next power phase.

Creative Expression, or synergy, means the ability to communicate in order to put into action our talents and skill sets. In this step we take a focused idea and seek a cooperative opportunity where there is a possibility to exchange energy between the two opposing energies. Creative expression is the causing of energy to flow between the two opposites so that a synergy can take place. Synergy is the result of two energies combining to form a third energy that is greater than the sum of the two individual energies.

Stage 4: Materialization.

Once you have a synergy then it's time to convert that synergy into the formation of something solid and tangible. It is the basis of manifestation or actualization. All actualization goes through a four step process. Everything created begins with an impulse. The impulse is the energy that propels an idea within us. To materialize this impulse we move through the four stages.

First an idea forms as a concept. From there, the next step is to bring the concept into a creative stage or clearly visualized plan. Once we have a plan, we can divide it up into tasks and apply resources, such as money, time and persons needed to accomplish each task. This is the third stage or execution stage. Finally we have a tangible result that has utility that can be of benefit to a third party. Thus our idea has been actualized and someone in the world will benefit.

Here is an example.

We enjoy taking a walk at the beach. However, after we have walked for a while we start to feel a nagging back pain. The pain in our back starts to become very noticeable. Suddenly, the pain (the pressure point that needs to be changed) triggers an idea within our mind's eye that we would like to have something on which to sit.

We hate sitting in the sand because it makes us feel sticky, so out of necessity (the mother of invention), we conceptualize a chair. Visualizing our sitting on a chair is just a concept, but immediately following the concept is an idea of a chair that we could design to take with us to the beach.

We also notice that there are many other people who might prefer to sit rather than stand; perhaps we have just hit on a commercial idea and a solution.

We then further conceptualize a portable lightweight chair that people can take with them, when they know they will be spending a long time at the beach.

From this concept stage, we start to create a plan that illustrates our chair in fine details. At this point we can either abandon our concept or we can continue. Many opportunities are often lost at this

stage because there is no ability to structure and then to execute the plan.

If we are able to follow through, (depending on our mental patterns); we will start to gather all the materials necessary to make a prototype of our chair. Once we have all the materials, we can assemble our chair into a working prototype and take it for a test, the next time we go to the beach. We may even want to show it to other beach goers and determine if there is any market for our brain wave.

The power of materialization is the process of bringing a concept into a physical reality. This is the basis of all human ingenuity and creation. Everything starts as a concept, forms into an idea, becomes a plan that can be broken into tasks and made ready for execution.

By understanding and completing the sequence, we can be more assured of completing the process and achieving the expected end result.

We see in our synchronous universe that all energy is made available to each part of the system and that each component part has the opportunity to cooperate with another opposing component in order to provide for a third or creative expression of the two components.

All this is done with the single unifying energy of

the entire system. In other words the universe is providing the energy for us to interpret and use.

The first four powers indicate that we are all part of a system that requires our human participation so that the system can endure.

First, we have the ability to form ideas;

Second there are others who will appreciate our ideas. There are always people or other entities with needs for which we have creative solutions. Through the power of cooperation we can create exchange, which is a flow of energy in the form of either better ideas, helpful people or even money.

Third, there needs to be a Creative Expression or spark that flows between the opposites so that some unique modification can take place that will provide value.

Fourth, as the flow continues from idea to creation and thereafter execution, something tangible will result. There is no real limitation to this process and in fact, there is an unlimited opportunity *if we just increase our awareness or expand our consciousness.*

Stage 5: Expansion

Once the newly created form has materialized, it immediately starts to change or morph into something other than its original form.

This change is the process of evolution as it causes the form to adapt or modify, primarily for the purpose of improving itself and raising its energy and consciousness to higher and higher levels. This evolutionary thrust applies to us as humans as well as to all our creative endeavors. We can grow and expand by understanding this stage and use the productivity gathered in the fourth stage to develop momentum.

The fifth stage is where we move out from ourselves and our creations to include and encompass other entities. In other words we reach out to the world around us in order to bring it into our sphere of influence for that which we have just created. We promote to our market, so to speak. We expand our materialization so that it can grow and enlarge our sphere of influence; the result maybe more money, more power, more relationships.

None of us is an island. We grow by expanding our awareness and influence and providing something that we have, to some other entity, so that the other entity will benefit. Since we are part of a synchronous whole, what is given up is immediately reciprocated by the Universe and in much stronger levels. The greater that our capacity is to give, so the greater is our capacity to receive.

We offer what we have developed in the fourth stage so we can expand in the fifth. We take what we have produced in the fourth and replicate it, or modify it, or expand it so that we can provide for more and more persons needing our contribution. This is the power of expansion. It is the natural outflow from the fourth stage. If the fourth stage is building a box, then the fifth stage is creating a window or a door out of that box.

Thus far we have gone through five stages. We draw our energy from a total energy field in which we are all connected and have our being. We then cooperate with seemingly diverse and opposing energies, so that we can continue to exist. This cooperation leads to a creative expression, or synergy, which is greater than the sum of the cooperating partners. In other words, communication takes place. The creative energy then leads to an impulse toward materialization because an idea needs to be formed into something of practical utility.

Ideas become actualized through the creative genius of the individual parts, whose genius is really an expression of the synchronous whole!

Ideas then change and evolve and mature, they reach out and influence until they are met with a counter force or even competing element.

Stage 6: Osmosis - Law of Response.

When we get to stage 6 we find ourselves interacting with the world in a way that was not possible up until this point in our evolution.

This is the stage where the power of osmosis "kicks in" because it is where we develop the ability to respond to the feedback from energies outside of our own.

While in stage 5 we started to morph into something greater than our original form, (we added windows to our box); in stage 6 we respond to the world outside of ourselves. We accept responsibility for the care and protection of other life forms and we seek out a harmony between ourselves and the universe.

This is where we discover balance and appreciate beauty, and as microcosms, we reflect the macrocosm within us. This is the stage where we learn the need to give back to society and the world in order to uplift it.

We now become aware of our social responsibility and discover the benefits of networking. We fully understand relationship roles and the concept of the team. Stage 6 development responds to the need to build success through osmosis. Osmosis is the pressure of a system to equalize through absorption.

For example, a high handicap golfer will play much better in a game with a low handicap golfer, than with another high handicapper. The high handicapper's game is lifted by the better player to a higher standard and somehow this rubs off on the high handicapper.

When we surround ourselves with successful people we will become more successful. Greatness leads to greatness and success builds success.

If the momentum for change that is developed in stage 5 can continue into stage 6, there is the opportunity to experience the "snowball effect".

One becomes magnetically charged and the universe responds fully to this magnetism. Beauty and abundance become attracted to us because we are resonating in harmony with the beauty and abundance of the universe. With the greater success possibility of stage 6, we must assume greater responsibility. If we have more power, we need to use it wisely. If we have more money, we need to spend it wisely. If we have good health, we need to tend to it more wisely.

Stage 6 is where individual creativity interconnects with universal creativity and opportunities abound, however always with the need for adjustment and a modified response.

Stage 7: Power Vision.

In stage 6 we interact with the macro forces and are exposed to forces greater than our own individual force. It is at this time when such an external force is reflected back upon ourselves that we learn to see with a "power vision". Our environment acts as a magnifier to increase our understanding.

This seventh stage vision is the vision brought about by self study. With this vision we learn to see into the depths of our own being. Here we can visualize clearly as we learn to remove our own egos and discard our judgmental view points. We become what we see because at this level of vision there is no longer a seer and a seen. Just the *seeing* is possible.

Not everybody is comfortable with the scrutiny of a stage 7 vision. All flaws and faults are revealed in the spotlight so that mistakes can be corrected. In stage 6 we learn to adjust to the world and in stage 7 we discover an understanding of how that adjustment can be used to improve our circumstances. Without the tyranny of ego to cause us suffering, we can endure our errors and discover the clarity that such a vision makes possible.

We learn to understand that instinct can be coupled with conscious awareness, which leads to very sharpened intuitive responses. At this level we can visualize an idea in all its details and energize our visualization so that we ourselves become cocreator of our world. The power of vision is our internal measurement system. We track all responses and make corrections. Here is where we learn the art of tweaking to become improved performers.

Stage 8: Co-creation.

When we reach stage number 8, we are ready to bring power to the world around us. We become power channels and are able to manifest our ideas with a sense of ease that was not possible before.

Here is where we "kick it up a notch" We have the opportunity to take spiritual energy and bring it to a physical plane so others can benefit from its practical application.

Richard Branson put together a concert for Bangladesh and Bono created a benefit program for sufferers of "aids" that became world recognized events. We can understand the enormity of the opportunity that a cocreator stage 8 can provide. Bill Gates is using his wealth to improve the health and life of countless millions of people. His ideas have attracted the wealth of Warren Buffet.

All these examples are of stage 8 cocreators. They have all developed the clarity and power vision in stage 7 and have manifested their vision into the next stage.

Each of us at our own level can be a creator and bring a real benefit to someone or something outside of our own little world and become cocreators of a better universe. Even if we help the life of just one person on the planet we will be doing the work of a cocreator. Stage 8 is therefore the stage of supercharged personal power.

When we realize that in terms of the universe we are just tiny specks of dust, walking around on a planet that is no bigger than a tiny speck of dust relative to the cosmos, it is hard to feel too important. Yet every tiny speck of dust is important, otherwise it would not be here.

Stage 9: Humility-The Sense of Gratitude.

In stage 9 we discover the enormity of the universe and the cosmic stage on which we play our little part. Stage 9 is the opportunity to surrender our egos and to merge into this enormity as a cosmic person. Now we can use all our skills to grow spiritually and to use whatever abundance we have gained as fuel for the NEXT cycle starting with 1 and unfolding through 9. Each cycle starts with new ideas, cooperation, creative expression, materialization, expansion, interdependence, power vision, cocreation and final merging into a bigger opportunity.

This final stage is where we have the opportunity to complete the process and discover liberation,

but it is here where we also discover that it is more beneficial to renew the cycle again and again until all our fellow earth citizens can enjoy liberation together. Until that day, we agree to continue to work for the total liberation of the entire world. This is our earthly purpose.

Liberation from disease and poverty and suffering; this is the liberation that we can experience for ourselves and which we must bring about for all mankind.

Here is the real irony and the take-away. By striving for the liberation of others, whether it is from poverty, bad health, a lack of education or whatever; we become liberated. By striving for the abundance of others, we receive abundance.

We are only on this planet for a blink of an eye. Our time may be limited to eighty or ninety years. One third of that time is spent sleeping. When we sleep we recharge. When we awaken, we need to take charge of the skills we possess to do something that will lead to our own growth and evolution and in turn contribute to the planet's evolution.

Why else are we here? Life is not a summer camp. Life is for the purpose of spiritual growth and the experience of a perfect, peace, profound.

Each one of us needs to take a good look in the

mirror, discover our talents and skills and use them to build a better and more rewarding life for all those who come into our field of influence, and therefore ourselves, in the process. In the process of creating abundance, we experience abundance.

Although the progress from Stage 1 to Stage 9 may seem like a saga only meant for the idealist, in truth it is the journey or pilgrimage that we all must make, and we do whether we are aware of it or not. Some of us may never achieve the financial status of a Bill Gates, but that is not the point. We are not Bill Gates. He has his own destiny to fill and we each have ours. The point is to proceed through the nine phases of growth, and to keep repeating the cycle over and over in an upward directional spiral. Again as we proceed through life, it is not the rewards that we focus on but the journey. The rewards are in the journey.

We have seen that by simply picking a target on which to focus, we can expand our consciousness and elicit the cooperation of the universe. By consciously working our way through the stages we acquire the benefits of the nine powers and become attuned to the Source of abundance. Therefore we never lack for anything.

Interestingly, the number 9 in a multiplication will always produce a number that returns to 9. For example, $9 \times 7 = 63$ and $6+3 = 9$. Another example;

$9 \times 50 = 450$ and $4+5+0 = 9$. No matter what number we multiply by 9, the result when reduced to a single digit will always equal 9. Nine is demonstrating that the flow of energy is constant and is never destroyed. As in the laws of physics, energy can only be transformed from one form into another. When we reach stage 9, completion, we get ready to start the cycle all over again but as a more evolved and wiser person. After 9 comes, 10 and 10 is $1+0$ or 1. So we start again but at a higher notch.

The 0 is a factor that remains hidden from our view all the way through our progress from stage 1 through 9. When we get to the second round starting at 10 we are now aware of the role of the 0 in our life. This is our connection to our own source; the source of our being and the source of our power and abundance.

Learning to harmonize and activate these stages in our life will bring a magnetic flow filled with abundance. Making this flow a habit is truly the way to a Master Mind.

Let us recap so far;

In part 1 – we discussed the foundation necessary to begin a complete overhaul of our mind patterns. These patterns originate from our own thoughts and actions that we make each and every day of our lives. Every thought we have will lead to an action, even if that action is to do nothing, because doing nothing is still an action.

The accumulation of all our thoughts and actions creates a reservoir of impressions or seeds with a potential to grow according to the information held within those seeds. An acorn has all the information stored within itself to produce an oak tree, given the right conditions of growth; namely soil, water, sunlight and time.

We are all aware that some things in life can be created and controlled by ourselves. For example, we can schedule a vacation, make the reservations, book the flight, call the taxi, go to the airport, board the plane and get to our destination, all as a result of some thought and planning.

Then there are the events that we seem to have no control over. Those are the times when the taxi gets a flat tire, we arrive at the airport late and we miss our flight.

But here is the question. Who is in control? Who is causing the events to unfold so that the taxi gets a flat? Who is causing us to miss our plane flight? Is it the taxi? Perhaps we can blame the tire manufacturer? Perhaps it was the construction worker who left the nails in the road that caused the hole in the tire? Who should take responsibility for our missing the flight?

Could it be our own fault? Perhaps we left home too late and never allowed for contingencies?

We could have left home early, which would have meant taking a different taxi, which would have missed the nails in the road and gotten us to the airport a little early. The drama would have unfolded differently.

However, we did not leave home early and we did hit the nails and we did miss the airplane. The reason this occurred is because we are directed by our habits or mind patterns. We make it a habit of leaving later in preference to sitting at the airport a little earlier and having to wait. This is our impatient, mind pattern that puts us in the same circumstance over and over again.

We need to identify these patterns and take action to change them so that we can get different results in the future. This is the lesson of Karma.

Secondly, we do not see the world as it is but rather as we perceive it to be. Everything experienced is first filtered through our prebuilt mind conditioning filters. We see the world as we want to see it or as we have been taught to see it but never as it is. We are therefore locked into a 'mind fog'.

First, our patterns need to change and second we also need to clear the mind fog so we can see clearly.

Our mind is fogged when we blame the taxi driver for getting the puncture that prevented us from getting to the airport. We feel all kinds of frustration and anger, we yell at the taxi driver for getting a puncture, (as if he did it on purposes) by not looking where he was going, and we become enraged at our failure and disappointment in not reaching our airplane on time.

Life often presents an irony for our learning. Later we find out that the plane we missed, took off and was forced to make an emergency landing in another city and all the passengers were transported to a hotel where they would have to spend the night, until the plane was repaired and could fly again in the morning.

All of a sudden, we thank our lucky stars or God for the taxi driver who caused us to miss the flight. He just went from being the lowest creature on the earth to an angel in about one hour. This is Mind Fog.

To be in the path of abundance, we have to change the patterns of Karma and clear the Fog. Can you imagine the dialog that would go on in our heads, if the airplane that we missed actually crashed, killing all onboard?

But there is more. We have to focus on the Truth. We earlier defined Truth as that which does not change. But since everything in creation changes and therefore, none of it, by definition can be called the "Truth", all of our world, including our mind and senses and ego is nothing other than a perception bound up in the "Mind Fog".

Yet there is an element within us, the "I" factor that is permanent. This is the objective witness that watches everything that we do. If I feel happy, the "I" factor can actually witness me being happy. So the person that is feeling the happiness is not the real "I" but the ego I. By learning to differentiate between the phantom ego that calls itself I, and the real I that is able to witness the entire life drama, we come to lose our fear of everything. Everything else besides the "I" factor is born, grows and then dies. The "I" factor alone remains permanent.

Now if I am the "I" factor and not the ego, I have just discovered who I really am and I have nothing to fear because I am permanent in a world of constant change. I don't die because I am not born. "I" is the sustaining power within life because it is the spark of life itself. All else is its projection.

So the take away from this lesson is that everything that happens to us is for a reason, and the reason is to reveal the "I" factor once and for all. What happens to us, is our fate or destiny, if we want to call it that, and how we respond to our fate, is our Free Will. We can choose to fight, or panic and retreat, or we can simply give up.

But we could also take the path of abundance. On this path, we do not blame anyone or anything, we simply change our bad habits for good; we replace poison arrows with love arrows. We stop being attached to our perceptions (ego) and rather seek the truth.

Then we integrate our ideas in sync with the world around us to provide benefits and service without concern for the rewards. The rewards will happen automatically.

The net result of this kind of action is a person who has intelligence and integrity. Who would not want to be around such a person?

The Path of Cognitive Action

Step 3 – Appropriate Action

In this section we move to a more definitive process, that we, as individuals, can undertake to prepare new habit patterns that will bring about a state of abundance.

In the previous section, we discussed the four step philosophical process needed to prepare our minds to create a certain way of thinking that is necessary to change the directional flow of thought from a more exoteric (outward oriented) to a more esoteric (inward oriented) direction.

In this section we will now build on that new way of thinking by developing the three main ingredients for success;

- motivation,

- inspiration,

- insight (clarity)

(Gut, Heart, Head); we need all three.

There are eight steps to undertake, together with a consequential ninth; each one is a separate step but integral to the whole process.

The steps are as follows:

- Vision
- Presence
- Passion
- Purpose
- Position
- Visualization
- Planned Action
- Connectivity
- Integration

The first four steps combine to produce motivation.

Vision

We begin with our vision. What is our vision? This is the essential question that needs resolution. If we don't have a vision, we are going to be stuck in a very dense mind fog for a very long time. We need a vision to give us purpose.

A vision is a dream that we have about how our reality could be and it becomes the basis of the patterns that we will bring to life, so to speak. If we have a vision that we can hold onto then we have something that behaves like a guide or a star track that keeps us on target. By holding onto our vision we program ourselves, often automatically, with the information that is necessary to keep us focused.

To grasp our vision we need to ask ourselves, what is the one thing in life we want to achieve?

To do this properly, we should start by asking the question this way. *If there is only one thing we can have in our life, what would it be?*

Many folks will often respond that there are many things in life they want to achieve. But the question is, *if there was only one thing in life we want to achieve what would it be?*

After we have answered this first question, we can then ask, what would be the second and then the third and so on. This prioritizes what is important to us.

Let us say that we decide that the most important thing in our life is to achieve a dream home for our family. Then, the next question we would ask is, what would be the number one thing we would like to achieve AFTER we have achieved our dream home? Usually, once we achieve something, immediately a new want creeps in and we're off to the races all over again.

Therefore we should develop a life vision that will

include many things along the way but which takes into account our deepest and innermost yearnings.

What would you like written on your epitaph? How about – "here lies a successful person who found abundance and gave abundantly to all those around him". How will **you** build abundance? Answer that question and you will know your vision.

Presence

Presence is the condition of *being here now*. Before any task can begin, we have to have a starting point. The only starting point is the point at which we are at in the present moment. Every journey begins with the first step and only when that first step is taken can we say we are on the way to realizing our vision.

No matter what we do, we should always do it from a point of concentration, otherwise the results become fragmented. Fragmentation occurs when we do not have total agreement between our different faculties. We have a left brain faculty, which is analytical and communicates in words, while we also have a right brain that is artistic and communicates in patterns. We have emotions which are the feelings we have at any one time and then we have a physical body that transmits and receives information back and forth.

If our right brain and left brain, emotions and physical body are all sending different messages, we are fragmented. Therefore, to be in the state of presence, our different faculties need to be gathered together to deliver one unified message. Only when this occurs do we have the power to bring about a new reality.

There is only one time when we have any control to concentrate our thoughts, actions and feelings, and that time is *now*, in the present moment.

Many of us have difficulty staying in the present moment because the mind can behave like a wild horse. Every sensory input we receive from one of our senses, or the recalling of something in our memories, can lead to a fragmentation of thoughts and feelings and a drifting into the past or the future.

Consider what happens when we drive to work. We get into the car, turn on the radio and forty five minutes later we arrive at our destination without the foggiest notion of what was going on along the way.

We thought a thousand different thoughts and took a thousand different meanderings in our minds, as we traveled, oblivious to our surroundings. This is a state of fragmented mindlessness and scattered energy, and we all suffer from this condition. In fact it is the nature of the mind to behave like a wild horse. It is our purpose to tame it.

What typically happens is that one of our senses will trigger a thought. Perhaps we pass a billboard with a picture of someone being pulled behind a boat on skis. The next thing we know, we are in memory lane remembering when we tried to ski on some river or lake twenty years ago. If that doesn't happen perhaps we find ourselves thinking of the next vacation we would like to take, in some other part of the world.

And it doesn't stop there; soon we see ourselves at the hotel, which reminds us of the last time we went on vacation and how we had a fight with the manager because our room wasn't ready. While we were talking to the manager his assistant, a gorgeous girl from Switzerland interrupted to say he had a phone call.

The girl reminded you of someone you met when you visited Lake Geneva as a teenager. She invited you to meet her friends and you remember the delicious sandwich you had at the little café on one of the quaint streets in Geneva.

In fact, now that you think of it, you feel like something to eat so perhaps you should stop off at the deli on the way into work and pick up a BLT, which reminds you to call the restaurant on Broad Street to make a reservation for Saturday night.

You tell yourself not to forget otherwise you will

be in the dog box because you promised your wife you would do it first thing this morning. You wonder why she couldn't make the booking knowing what a hectic day at the office you are going to have. You start to think about your presentation…..and on and on and on!

Not once are we being mindful of our surroundings or focused in the present moment. When we finally arrive at work we have no idea of what was going on along the way. How much mental energy did we waste on mindless day dreaming on the way to work? But take heart, we all are guilty of these mental excursions.

Presence is a state of *mindfulness*. This is a condition which requires that we mind each moment to the full.

Try this little exercise. Set a timer, or watch the second hand on your watch for one minute. Then either feel your pulse on your wrist, or watch the second hand move for 60 seconds, without allowing any other thought to intrude for the duration of the full sixty seconds.

The chances are that you will not be able to do this exercise at all, without any other thought interfering. This is the nature of our restless mind.

Three little words will help us to remember to practice

mindfulness. They are BE HERE NOW. Once we are in the present moment we can focus on a task at hand and apply creative energy to accomplishing the task by using more mind and brain power than if we are scattered in six different directions.

Now is the only time we have. We may not be alive tomorrow. Therefore we need to do whatever we intend doing, NOW. If we consider the urgency of only having this time now in which we can do something, we are much more likely to take action instead of procrastinating. The opportunity is now. If we wait, we may just miss it altogether.

Another thing about presence is the experience of being more alive. When someone is truly in the now, they have an expanded presence because they are more fully concentrated and energized. This gives the person more power, one that is perceived as charisma. When one is in control of the moment, others are drawn into that person's presence and are strongly influenced by it.

Some people just walk into a room and their presence is immediately felt. These are usually very, focused people and they are focused in the moment. They have all their faculties functioning fully and in agreement. They are in a state of 'paying attention'.

Interestingly, in order to be focused in the now, it

would seem as if we have to use so much energy to concentrate that we would tire very quickly. The opposite is true because the mental energy leakage is plugged and therefore, there is no waste of mental energy. Mindfulness can put one into an immensely relaxed state.

I have had many people tell me how tired they feel because of the incessant nagging that goes on in their minds. It feels to them like a day spent with screaming children.

Meditation practice is a great remedy for this condition because during meditation, we practice one-pointedness or concentration. We bring ourselves to the task at hand, which may be listening to our heart beat or chanting a mantra or riding on our breath, as it flows in and out of us.

The basis of all self motivation though, is to start with being in the present moment. Once we are present minded we cannot be absent minded and therefore we cannot be distracted by other non motivating thoughts.

An important aspect of staying in the now is having something to hook us or engage our attention. We need something we are interested in doing. That is why the next step in motivating ourselves to stay focused is, Passion.

Passion

Passion is all about the love of doing something. Passion is putting our heart and soul into an activity for no other reason than it is the only thing we want to do.

For some of us it is easy to be passionate because we have discovered something in life that captivates us and that is how we want to occupy our time. But for those of us who have not been captivated, we have a different problem. We may find ourselves doing things we don't really enjoy, and therefore we build up, on a subconscious level, high levels of frustration and even anger.

For those of us with this problem, we need to reinvent ourselves so that we can reinvigorate passion. A life with no passion is like a library with no books; a beautiful room but one that is vacated.

Passion is the ability to think with your heart. One of the great problems within our society today is that we have become too cerebral. Everything is a matter of rules and regulations and analysis. Where is the fun?

Passion is putting fun to work in our lives. We must have fun doing something because there is nothing that is so serious or important that prevents life from being enjoyed.

I would rather have brain surgery performed on me by a surgeon who is having fun while operating, rather than someone who is not enjoying himself.

Life is not always as accommodating as we would like it to be. We have our Karma to work out and in case you have forgotten, Karma is the law of cause and effect.

If we find ourselves in a situation that is devoid of passion, then remember the song by Crosby Stills and Nash – "if you can't be with the one you love, then love the one you are with". In fact this is such an important concept because *it is possible to become passionate about many things in life.*

Life is for working out our Karma and clearing the Mind Fog so that we can connect to Truth and experience abundance.

If we approach life with an attitude of gratitude rather than expectancy, then we will discover that we can be passionate about many things. The point is not to believe that there are only one or two things to be passionate about.

We are in control of our attitude to life. The object is to have fun and bring passion into our lives. It is impossible to find abundance without first finding passion.

If we have a natural passion for something; let's

say we love taking photographs, then that is the first activity to explore to see whether it is possible to pursue a life involved in some way with photography.

If we have specific skills, then those are the areas of least resistance in our life and the first ones to explore to find a life vocation. Usually we enjoy doing what we are good at. We <u>can</u> find something we are passionate about, whether it's what we love doing or whether it is a natural inborn talent or skill set that we possess. And we can pursue that with all vigor.

If we use our natural talents then we are contributing to the universal plan, otherwise we would not have acquired those skills. There are no accidents. Everything happens or exists for a reason.

Purpose

Why do we do the things that we do? If we never find our true purpose, we will find ourselves drifting from one kind of an activity to another.

If that is the case, we need to stop and take inventory. We need to catch our breath and say "this is what I am good at" or "this is what I love doing" and then be creative in finding ways in which to engage ourselves in those areas. We are much more likely to be successful doing the things that we love to do or are good at doing.

When we find success in an activity, we tend to pursue that activity with much more diligence because we believe we can be even more successful. Success breeds success. The combination of an easy flowing, (easy to do) activity, devoid of struggle, with a high level of enjoyment is a sure sign of a true purpose. One owes it to oneself to create the conditions to bring this level of purpose and passion together.

For example, my passion is the search for truth and the discovery of a purposeful life. I love the search more than anything and it has occupied my time for the last forty years.

Until recently, I had never considered my passion and purpose as a vocation (calling) to share with other people the extraordinary ideas and teachings I have received. I spent twenty years of my life as a real estate developer, which was an occupation I really enjoyed and which I was successful at doing. However, that occupation never really catered to my philosophical bent. Now, I realize the importance of making a paradigm shift in my personal life to include my passions in everyday activities. It makes each day an exhilarating day.

When one gets the "aha" experience or if one gets the feeling that nothing can go wrong, it is as if the stars are totally aligned. Then one gets a taste of the true purpose of life. That little taste may only be a short glimpse, but it is a life changing event.

Life is sometimes compared to living inside a dark room. We bump and thump our way through it, stubbing our toes here, knocking our heads there, and eventually we learn to navigate the obstacle course. If we are talented, we quickly learn to adapt to our surroundings and even become comfortable, as "champions of the darkness."

But with a little flip of the light switch the darkness is gone forever. No more thumping and bumping. This is the path of enlightenment.

When our vision, our passion, our purpose combine together in the present moment we feel truly motivated and can be properly positioned to go from the stage of motivation to the stage of inspiration. We even set ourselves up to experience the serendipity moment.

Our life purpose is to be a purposeful human being. It doesn't matter what we choose to do. We just need to bring our energy into the moment, have fun, and execute with a purpose. Even though we have a vision, a magnetic pull toward manifesting that vision, we must retain our sense of spontaneity. This happens when we live in the present moment.

In the present moment, we are not planning, we are

not slaves to plans that we must achieve or otherwise think we have failed. No, in fact we need to be light-hearted with a sense of humor. We need to laugh at our own seriousness, which in the global scheme of things is nothing more than a joke. We can never take ourselves too seriously. We need to be like dancers, enjoying the moment of music in our lives and we must always let the musical score be the vision that we hold within us. Remember the bumper sticker, "Man plans and God laughs".

Our attitude should be to be the best that we can be. That's it. Just be the best that we can be. Then whatever we tackle will be easy to accomplish. We have to tune-in to the universe, that 'one note' in which we are as part of the big picture. And we need to learn to dance; the dance of immortality, of an ever free spirit in ecstasy.

If one's Karmic patterns are aligned with one's purpose then reaching one's target will be easy. Sometimes though, our Karmic patterns are not aligned and we have to exercise a lot of will in order to pursue our goals. This is a test that is designed to strengthen our resolve. It is like doing a thousand sit-ups each day with weak stomach muscles; a total struggle. However, with persistence and resolve, our stomach muscles strengthen and the task can be accomplished.

The idea is to stay with the appropriate action plan

each and every moment, with no thought of the future results or the past occurrences. Being in the now is all that counts because it is only in the now that we have any control.

The next four steps have to do with Inspiration. In this second stage we convert all our motivation into inspiration. It is like converting potential energy into kinetic energy.

Posture (Position)

The first four steps have to do with self motivation, being energized at the gut level.

First, we have a vision of what our ideal should be, then we realize that there is a sense of urgency and the need to be in a state of presence. We know that now may be the only opportunity to do something. Next, there is passion, which means doing something because that is what we enjoy doing. Finally we apply purpose or intent, which is the drive to get on with our life as a purposeful person.

The next stage is to take a position. Position is how we feel about something. It is our position in regards to the task at hand.

Are we confident? Are we focused? Are we properly aligned? How is our posture, both physical and mental?

When we take a position, we take a stand. To stand for something means adopting a particular value or belief system, as long as that belief system is not delusional. That's why, in the first section of the book, we explored the fundamental four philosophical foundations of Truth that everybody, no matter what race, creed, sex or color can adopt. These four foundations remove delusional thinking that we have either been taught or have picked up along the way.

It has often been said that if we don't stand for something, we will fall for anything.

I know for example, what I stand for. I know that now is the only time I may ever have to take action, and that I am having fun because I love doing what I am doing. I also have a purpose or intent to do the best that I can in pursuing my personal vision.

In order to maximize one's power, it is helpful to study the way of martial arts or yoga. These Eastern disciplines are fully developed for bringing the mental and physical energy to a point for maximum effect.

For example, in Karate, one is taught to bring the Ki energy to the navel area through breathing and concentration. When the Ki is focused at this point, we can strike with maximum effect.

Try walking up the stairs, and as you do feel that you have a large energy reservoir in your navel area, and that as you climb, it is this energy that is propelling you as you up the stairs. I guarantee you will be amazed at the result. Just the thought of having a propelling energy, centered in the naval area, can make a profound difference as to how easy or difficult the task is.

Good physical posture is very important for many reasons. A person who walks tall, chin up, eyes focused on a target will have a more commanding aura about them than someone who walks around in a slouch.

By remaining aware of our posture we can channel the energy better and more efficiently throughout our psycho-physical system.

The combination of a strong mental and physical posture leads to better results in achieving our targets. Here again, we need to bring our left brain, right brain, feelings and body into a state of coordinated action.

Visualization

As part of the process of developing inspiration, visualization has no peer. It is the single most significant action we can take to accomplish or manifest our vision.

The understanding that we should have is that accomplishing our vision is more about us creating it, rather than reaching it. The reason so many people don't achieve their dreams is because they think that the object of their dreams exists somewhere out in the world and all they have to do is to go out, fight all the diverse elements and collect the prize. If we grasped the section on Mind Fog, we now know that it is **what is in our mind** that makes our reality and not something outside of us.

Visualization is the act of creating the result we seek, in our own mind, in all its detail, so that for us it already exists. Then it is just a matter of time before it will manifest.

Visualization is seeing with the mind's eye. It takes some practice; especially for those of us who might not see in pictures.

It is important to see the final result in all its detail. For example, the architect who is designing a house has to see each angle, each viewpoint, and each perspective. She has to visualize standing in a room and feeling the proportions, where the furniture is placed, the colors on the walls and so on. If she can do this with enough depth and intensity, it is just a question then of drawing the plans.

In fact we are architects of our own destinies. If we can visualize our vision and write it down in all its details, or draw it in pictures, very often someone else will actualize it for us and deliver it to us. This is the magic of creating a magnetized field of attraction.

Action Plan

In the first four steps we built motivation.

In the fifth step we adopted a posture of success. We channeled our energy, worked on a success attitude and now we feel unstoppable. Then in the sixth step, we visualized our vision. We actually saw ourselves being in possession of or living our dream. This strong visual is followed by the execution phase, which is our action plan.

The best way to accomplish something is to make it as clear as possible. We do this by removing all confusion and noise. Noise is the overwhelming amount of irrelevant information, from other people or places, that we receive constantly. These are all of life's distractions and we need to remain focused on our vision or goal. This does not mean not caring about others. In this instance I am talking about focusing on one's personal vision rather than being side tracked by other people's visions.

If we are building a business then we need to follow our business plan and only seek information pertaining to the stage of the business plan upon

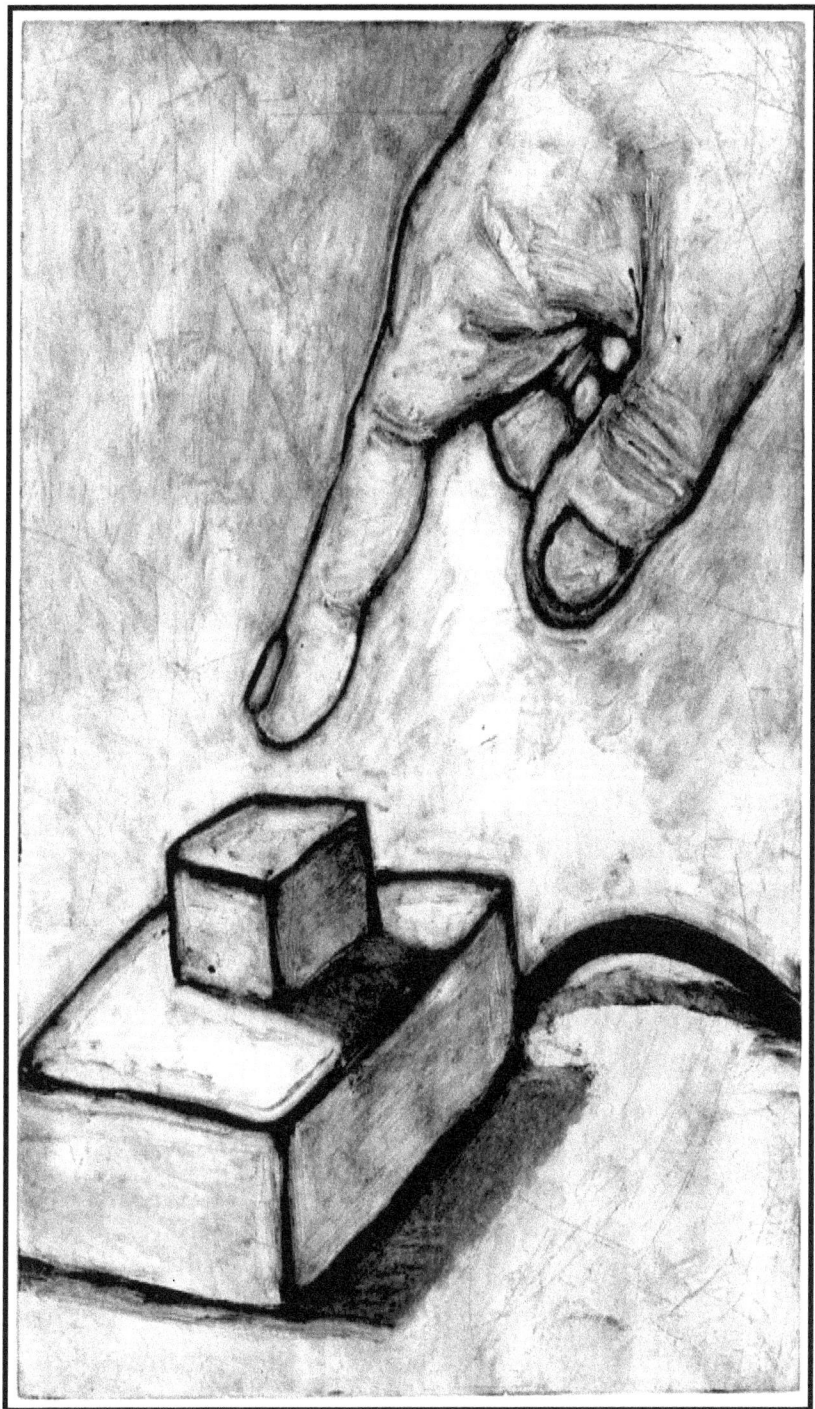

which we are focusing. If it's a relationship then again, we need to focus all our attention on the other person and resist distractions from other people. We need to be giving our best shot to whatever we are attempting to do.

We need to discriminate very carefully in regard to what information we allow through our filters. If the information furthers our cause or enhances our vision, we should take it, even pay for it when appropriate. However, if it is just a case of gathering encyclopedic information just for the sake of knowing about something, then it is best left alone. We should only obtain information when we need it. We need to filter out the hype and gossip that constantly creeps in to our awareness and which causes us to become diffused. Most people are afraid not to watch television or read the news. Why? This is an important question. Please try to answer it for yourself.

Suppose your goal is to repaint your house. Would you go out and buy two truckloads of bricks, because someone knows that you are upgrading your home and therefore decides to make you an offer for bricks; one that you can't refuse.

Just because you are in a renovation mode does not mean that you have to know everything there is to know about renovating. If you are not going to change the pavers why would you gather information or buy bricks for which you do not have immediate use?

Taking action means taking APPROPRIATE action. The wrong action will produce the wrong results. Taking no action will produce nothing.

A clear way to become action oriented is to break any task down into the smallest possible steps that make sense. We need to make a habit of creating a meaningful task list each day that will cause us to get that day's job done in the most efficient manner. It is not how hard we work but how smart we work.

So many people undertake a task that is too big and therefore it never gets done. The best way to eat an elephant, I am told, is one small bite at a time.

If we have small manageable tasks, that form a part of our visualized image, and if we have developed the right attitude or posture, then all we have to do is DO IT. Don't worry about the result. Just do it. Nothing ever gets accomplished from the fence. Even if the action does not work out as it should, there is always the possibility of doing it again.

As long as the task is a necessary one, small enough to manage and approached with the right attitude, it is almost impossible not to be successful at completing the task.

AND NOW COMES THE BIG TRICK.

We have to ingrain into our minds the correct pattern that makes the execution of the necessary tasks a daily habit.

Remember in our discussion concerning Karma, we discovered that the patterns or seeds that grow and manifest are the ones that produce the experience that we call our life.

So now, as part of our action plan, we need to create those seeds or habits that will produce that experience that is in line with our Vision. If we visualize properly, with the right approach and at the same time, if we break down our actions into small manageable tasks, and REPEAT this process DAY AFTER DAY for just 30 days, we will have formed new patterns that will act as channels of magnetic energy. They will attract to us the reality that we have visualized. The tasks must be a part of the total vision.

Imagine a five thousand piece jig-saw puzzle. First, we follow the picture (vision) on the box. We intend to frame this puzzle once it is completed, so that we can give it to someone as a gift, which is our (purpose). We then approach the puzzle (task) with enthusiasm (good posture), which we can easily do because we love doing puzzles (passion).

In order to complete the puzzle, we take one small piece at a time and try to fit it into the overall picture in our minds eye. We start with the corners, and then look for all the straight edge pieces (technique).

A useful little acronym for this stage is ACT. We must act by *Applying Consistent Technique.* If each day, we apply consistent technique, then, in no time at all, the task will be done.

The word 'Apply' means making the right effort, 'Consistent' means regularity and with equal pressure and 'Technique' means with a certain methodology.

Once we act, a result is assured. If we have proper visualization and appropriate action, we are doing all that we can to bring about our vision.

If something gets in the way and we are confronted with obstacles, as we will surely be, then we resort to our attitude (posture), make sure we channel our energy accordingly, and keep going. If we have negative Karma in the way, then the way to act appropriately is by constantly replacing poison arrows in our quivers with love arrows and resetting the patterns in our subconscious minds.

If things do not go so smoothly, we don't start firing poisonous arrows because we are frustrated. If we do, we will start the cycle of negative Karma all over again. By offering love in our relationships or service in our business, we position ourselves for the best possible outcome.

Connectivity

All of what we have done so far has been about ourselves and our vision. How we build motivation, and how we develop inspiration. Actually we have one more step in the inspiration phase and that is 'connectivity'.

We cannot achieve our vision in isolation of the rest of the world. We cannot be an island. We must interrelate to others. We cannot be doctors and practice medicine without any patients. Our patients are our connection to our vision.

If you remember, we discussed in the ten power steps, the number 2 and the number 6 stages. These two phases dealt with cooperation and osmosis, respectively. First we learn to cooperate and later we experience the uplifting pressure from connecting with success. We create a vision and the universe responds to it. This is connectivity.

We go about forming relationships, master mind groups, teams, and as a group mind we are better than any single mind in the group. There is a natural synergy.

The key to working in a team or group is to keep focused on your own vision. The purpose of the team is to help bring about the realization of your vision, which is something that may not be possible on our own.

Your team, or group, will kick your efforts into higher gear. One of the interesting attributes of working in a group is the blending of energies that is required to make the group work. You, as a leader of a group, have to be like bamboo; strong but resilient. You have to bend but not break. Bamboo is a perfect example of these attributes.

It is always helpful to listen. Connectivity means learning the art of listening. One cannot make progress if one cannot listen.

It is often the other points of view that will help iron out the wrinkles in our own ideas. What counts is that your vision is being executed upon and that the whole group is benefiting. Individual motivation has now been transformed into inspiration and the result that we achieve is the final outcome of having a strong vision.

Insight

Insight is a most interesting concept. The word insight means 'clear perception'. It also means 'self awareness' and the ability to understand and find solutions to personal problems. Insight suggests a solution. With insight there is no doubt. We have the solution.

Insight can also mean 'imminent'; something

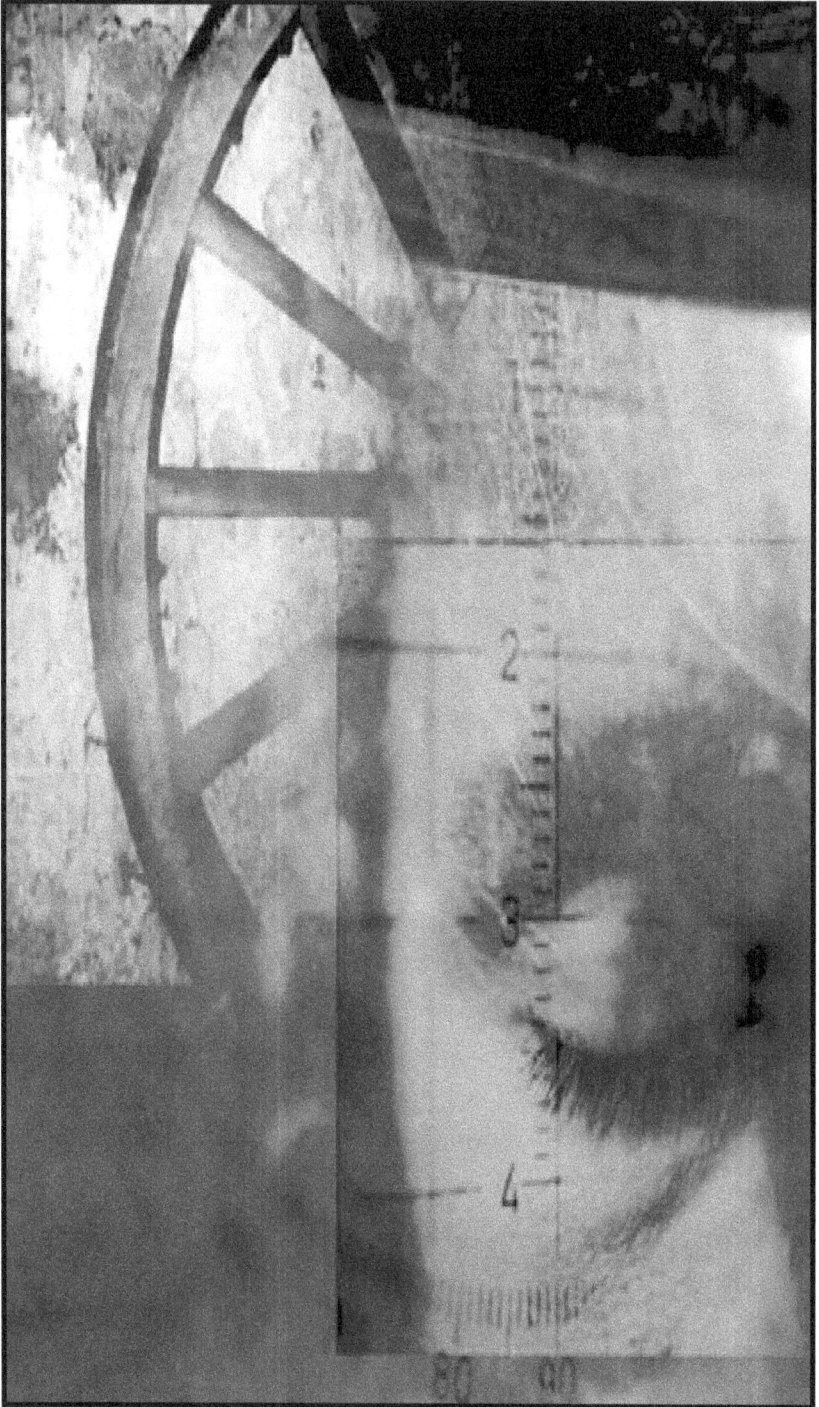

approaching, on the way, just around the corner within reach. If we have insight, it means our vision and our goals are now within reach and are tangibly close.

Our Motivation and our Inspiration merge into a single unifying experience called Insight. When we reach the stage of Insight, we have no more doubts. We have a clear vision of what is possible and what is real. We know that our reality is something we make for ourselves and we have no other choice but to keep unfolding our vision.

We experience the power of abundance by being in the state of abundance. We have found abundance because abundance has found us. The Universe has endowed us with a gift. We should cherish it and appreciate it.

In the final analysis abundance can mean something material and something spiritual. We should not be attached to the material because, as with all things material, it is either taken away from us or we are, at the end, taken away from it.

On the other hand our spiritual growth, gaining insight into the "I" factor is the permanent reward and one that becomes abundantly clear as we adopt and practice the philosophy of Truth and the goal of insight, as set out in this book.

Putting it all together

A Short Summary

One of the goals of this work is to find a formula that can help us to structure our thinking and to prepare us to have the best chance of achieving success in life.

All people, the world over, are pretty similar. We all want the basics in life; food and shelter, nice things, loving relationships, recognition and the ability to do something worthwhile. We all want to be healthy, wealthy and wise. We all want and need love. We all want to be free. Free from suffering and free to do our own thing.

In many cases, we are our own worst enemies. Either we have adopted the wrong ideas about correct living or we have been taught to take things on faith without the possibility of ever knowing if they have any validity.

Putting Our New Mindset to Work

When it comes to getting up in the morning and going out into the world to make our way, no matter if we offer a service or a product, whether we are artists or scientists, whether we operate from faith or from reason, or if we do all those things, ***we need to*** *exchange value with other people.*

All of life's endeavors, no matter what they are, require us to have the ability to inspire others, whether it's with our affections, our ideas or some product or service.

With the new understanding of "Mind," we discover that there is no pushing or pulling involved. There is, rather, the power of attraction. To activate this power, we need to clear the path of delusional thinking, learn to be natural and to take appropriate action.

In essence we need to BE – HERE – NOW so we can ACT. The power to do something requires us to gather all our energy, get started and keep going. If we follow our gut and our heart and apply a little head, we will be in fine shape.

Remember, the best way to overcome an obstacle is to move our consciousness to a point where the obstacle does not even exist. This is a deeply held spiritual secret that has been passed down through the ages. By changing from where we usually operate to a different level of being, the problems that once plagued us will evaporate from our lives, simply because they don't belong to our new level of consciousness. In summary, there are three parts to our effort.

Part A. – Embrace a New Belief System

Step 1. Use the Law of Cause and Effect

We must accept that all our actions will produce a reaction. Therefore, if we have a vision or a map, we must start our journey by taking the first step. We need to step aside from fear and just do it.

We begin and we continue. Every action we take is the kind of action needed to enliven the vision that we hold in our hearts and heads. If we are aiming at buying a house then we take all the steps necessary to achieve the purchase of a house.

We do not go looking at boats or motorcars or vacations. Those are the tests put there to sidetrack us from our intended target, which in this case is a house.

If we want to grow an oak tree, we must plant an acorn and not a date seed. Along the way, we must also take only those actions that are helpful to others in the process. We must constantly load our quivers with love arrows.

Step 2. Disassociate from our false perceptions.

We need to always remember that what we perceive is just our own perception. Knowing this, we can accept the opposite point of view to our own. We can then be free to anchor our thoughts to our real

center as opposed to our false ego.

Our ego will lead us deeper and deeper into the Mind Fog. We need to stand aside and behave like the witness; unattached to our emotions and our desires and impulses that constantly sidetrack us.

We need to attach to our vision and stay focused on that vision until we achieve its realization. Then, we can move on to the next and the next. Of course each step of the way could be a vision nested within a greater vision.

For example, let's say our vision is to become a doctor because we want to heal the broken people of our society. However, our first vision is to gain acceptance into a good medical school and to do this we need to gain good grades in our undergraduate program. Each grade can be a vision in a greater vision and so on. By accomplishing each vision, in its appropriate time, we succeed. Simple as that.

Step 3. Anchor to the Truth.

As we approach our vision and visualize it more and more each day, we need to understand that this vision is energized by a force that is responsible for producing such a vision. This is the central Truth of our own being and is at the center of our universe. We need to bring all our energy into this one point so that we can gather as much energy as possible to accomplish our goals. We should even eat correctly so that we take in food that provides us with energy rather than eat food which depletes it. We need to calm our minds and find the still point within us so that we can tap into an infinite supply of creative energy. This is the point of non duality or the point between two thoughts. We need to watch vigilantly for this point of stillness. This is the point where energy abounds.

Step 4. Exercise our Free Will.

This is the step where we do what is necessary to fulfill our vision, no matter what it takes, as long as it does not harm others. If we want the universe to assist us in achieving our goals, we need to provide assistance to the universe in turn. This is done by helping and serving others so that they can achieve their goals. Miss this step and we find ourselves alone and without the support of the world around us. If our desires are fulfilled through the benefitting of others then we are automatically creating love arrows for our Karmic quivers. These arrows will have positive effects on our own development as they ripen into the circumstances of our lives. Appropriate actions are those actions needed to reach our targets, step by step.

Part B. Understand the Terrain

Once we embrace the above four concepts, we become ready to harmonize with the natural steps of the universe, as it grows and evolves. In keeping with the natural rhythms of life, we maximize our energy and are swept along with the tide. Is it better to swim against the current or with it? As long as we swim with nature and not against it, we will find that we are made whole, i.e. we are healed. Direct experience will prove this to us, so it is worth making the effort. In the beginning it will feel like we are swimming against the tide but that is because we have become perverted to what is natural.

Growth energy is symbolized by the process of numeration from 1 to 9.

Step 1- Focus:

First we tune into the universal energy and understand that we are all connected. Because of this connectedness, we can focus on our vision and the entire universe will respond to energize the vision for us. So step 1 is to focus on our vision.

Step 2 - Polarity:

The next step is to recognize any polarizing energy or opposition energy to ours. This is polarized energy that creates an opposite terminal, such as in a battery. Only when there are two opposing terminals in the battery can a current flow. We discover this opposing terminal in our lives by finding out what others want or need. This is usually opposite to what we want.

For example, if I want to sell you my book, then that is what I want. However, if I specifically try to solve your need then that is what you want. In order for energy to flow, I must solve your need. Therefore I must focus on providing a benefit to someone else instead of seeking the benefits for myself.

As energy is focused, it develops along the lines of the person who is focusing the energy. Once that energy builds up, it will need an outlet and that outlet is the person who is in need of something that the newly focused energy can provide.

Step 3 – Synergy:

By finding out what someone else needs and conjoining that need with the ability to satisfy that need, we are creating a synergy. This is what we do in step 3. We find a creative expression resulting from two opposing needs. The outcome is a creative solution and is understood by both parties, as a win - win situation. The universe is improved and expanded as a result.

Step 4 – Structure:

The creative expression, needs cultivation in

order to go from idea to actuality and manifest its full potential. Just as the acorn needs soil, water, sunshine and time, so does our effort in this fourth step. We need to take all our ideas, visualize each step, create plans and tasks, apply energy and effort until each task is completed and then keep repeating the steps until the entire process is complete. It does not matter if some steps have to be repeated; nobody is judging.

Step 5 - Expansion.

Once we have a completed process, an actualized solution, we are ready to introduce the result to the world and use it to benefit as many other people as possible. In this step we are promoting the synergy achieved in step 3 and the result of the synergy created in step 4. Whatever it is, it has value. We need to offer our unique value as a contribution to as many people in the world as we can with the pure intention of helping and improving the world.

Step 6 – Reciprocity:

In step six we experience the reciprocity between us and the world outside of ourselves. Here we gain a response from our efforts. We take heed of the response and accept our responsibility to find harmony amongst all the diversity that is outside of ourselves. We adjust and integrate our vision into the diversity and thereby establish a position for our creativity amongst a larger and more diverse group of interests.

Step 7 - Analysis:

We learn to analyze all the reactions that we receive in a way that will increase our awareness of the needs of others. As a result we can create more opportunities to provide even better solutions. Self examination of our perceptions and responses lead to a deeper and more comprehensive understanding about the process of growth and prepares us for greater levels of achievement.

Step 8 – Power:

We are now in the position to build a real and enduring enterprise that will be available to others on an ongoing basis. We have taken our ideas and refined them so that they can be used by others to improve their situations. We are at the stage of bringing creativity to materiality and can even monetize our creativity by accepting money as a medium of exchange. In the same way this process applies to relationships where we focus on love, learn to give unconditionally, and work together to provide security in the form of food, shelter, clothing, belonging, socializing, and even the opportunity for actualizing more creativity.

Step 9 – Gratitude:

We are humbled by the universal acceptance of our creativity and are filled with gratitude that the universe is responding to us by providing a state of abundance, in reciprocation for our participation as a cocreator of value to others. We understand the need and urgency to create abundance for others by helping to remove their obstacles, or by supplying energy in the form of money, ideas, spiritual direction and other growth mechanisms.

Step 10 – Cycles:

We repeat steps 1 through 9, establishing our energy and efforts in the formation of an "abundance mindset". This mindset is developed as a result of our acceptance of the four foundations of our new mindset philosophy, as outlined in Part A, and the ten stages of growth in Part B.

Part C: Actions

Step 1 – Vision:

We explore, write down and tune into our vision. We start by discovering our natural skill sets and talents. We take into account the things we love to do, and which come easy to us. We understand these passions and skills as the basic tools for building our vision of our own reality, which we know must be converted into an actuality. Then we turn our attention to the one thing in life we would like to do if we had no restrictions. We ask ourselves what is the one thing we would do if we absolutely knew we could not fail.

Step 2 – Passion:

Our vision is a labor of love. This is what we want to do or bring about for no other reason than it is what we love to do. We learn to think with our hearts and feel with our heads. We love our dream and we believe in it. We awaken our passion to the unfolding of our vision. In the beginning, we may have to psyche ourselves into the state of passion. Passion is just an attitude. Depending on our habit patterns, we may have to revisit our approach to life. We may even have to pick ourselves up by our own bootstraps. But once we do, we find ourselves with a new momentum based on a new attitude and a revived passion. We all have passion in us. We may just need to jump start it.

Step 3 – Presence:

We recognize that the opportunity to dream and unfold our vision on the world is only available to us now. There is no future and the past no longer exists. We therefore take responsibility to act now. Being alive in the present is the only time that we have. It is where all the opportunities exist. There is no opportunity to go back into the past and relive it. The past has truly gone. It is time for spontaneous action. This requires that we focus on a single point called the NOW.

In the same way there is no future. Time does not work in a linear mode. It may seem that way but that is a false perception. Our vision exists only in the present moment. If we behold our vision with all its details, that beholding can only take place in the NOW. Our reality is NOW. We have to learn to live in our reality and not in past memories or future fantasies.

Step 4 – Purpose:

We examine the purpose of our vision to be sure that it integrates with our purpose as a human being. We all have a purpose and that purpose is to be "spiritually awake" human beings. But each one of us needs to express our purpose according to our own nature and our own particular characteristics.

We must accept that we are not born on this earth to waste a life. We are needed by the universe to fulfill a higher purpose even if our purpose may seem insignificant to us. A watch without the smallest, most insignificant spring cannot function. There are no superfluous parts in the universe, not one. So even with a vision and a passion and the urgency to live and manifest it now, we still need to feel a sense of purpose; our "raison d'être".

We are born into this life to find ourselves and to remember who we really are; to pursue self realization and to experience unity with our Source. In this process is the paradox of life, because the entire universe exists to help us achieve this purpose and at the same time, we are endowed with a creative talent to contribute to the creation of the universe. We are the eyes and the ears, the hands and the feet , the soul of evolution. Our job is to create a universe in which all the souls can remember their unity with their source. This truly is a Divine Purpose.

Step 5 - Posture:

We strengthen our posture, both physically and mentally. We have a vision, we are making it real NOW, because we love it, and we will not allow anybody else to talk us out of it. We take a firm position mentally because we have listened to our heart's desires and accepted our purpose with all the logic and rationale of our heads. We are so motivated that we know, at a gut level, that our vision is right for us. We stand firm, we look ahead, and we are prepared to take the necessary steps. We fear nothing because we have nothing to fear. We are finely tuned and ready to play our note, for us the most important note in the one song.

Step 6 – Image in Action.

We carry our vision in our minds and in our hearts. We meditate to clear our minds of extraneous thoughts so that only our true vision remains. We constantly clear the jungle to reveal the castle of our creative dream, our vision. We visualize our vision in as fine a detail as possible. We learn that imagination is our greatest tool once we hone it to work for us instead of against us. We take imagination and turn it into "image in action." We instill this vision into our being and create it as a Karmic pattern. We do this by stilling our minds to the point of quietness where we can encounter our own center of power; our power to bring forth our dream is at its maximum at this center.

Step 7 - Action:

We use our learning and experience, our brain power, to scientifically plan each piece of our vision by breaking it down into small manageable steps or projects. Then we apply all our resources to accomplish each step in our dream puzzle. As each step is completed, we feel a positive affirmation that our vision is processing fully. We know beyond all doubt that our vision is already manifested, it now only needs full materialization. And through our motivation and inspiration we have assured the cooperation of the universe.

Step 8 – Blending:

We now connect with others in terms of understanding that we alone cannot create anything. Each one of us is in partnership with the universe, which may come in the form of a single other person, or a contribution from a million other people. Therefore we are flexible, we bend but we do not break. We are like the bamboo – strong, firm and flexible. We know we are not islands. We have learned to be independent in our thinking, and we have learned to be interdependent with each other and the universe around us. We blend with our world, with nature and the universe, then we offer our contribution for the improvement of all.

Step 9 – Insight:

By this stage we have absolute clarity that we and the universe are a single entity. We are a note in a single song. This is the ultimate state of abundance because we become the **abundance** through the proper understanding of our mind patterns, our perceptions, our anchoring to our own power center and the appropriate actions needed to unfold our visions as cocreator of the universe. It is the most wonderful and exciting realization of who we really are.

We have embraced a philosophy of truth, we have learned to harmonize with what is natural and we have taken appropriate actions to map out and manifest our visions. What remains is the need to take the opportunity that each day offers us and to step fully into the present moment, each step without fear. In this way we can all awaken to enjoy our greater reality.

Conclusion

In our society, everybody wants the power to have more choices. Choices come with having enough money. But money alone is not sufficient. And money will never be there for us, if our mindset is not set properly. With a proper mindset we can attract abundance, whether abundance is in the form of money or any other intangible desire.

It all starts by being curious. We need to be curious about how our lives work; curious enough to want to change from being a passenger in life to being a driver. We need curiosity to find new ways of generating ideas that have value and we need curiosity to create a new mindset for ourselves.

Above all we need to accept the responsibility to create an abundance or an "abundance mindset" for ourselves. We should never expect others to do it for us because nobody else can. It is truly up to each one of us.

How can we help others if we have not learned to help ourselves?

Rudyard Kipling, in his "Just-So" stories, said;

I keep six honest serving men

(They taught me all I knew);

Their names are What and Why and When

And How and Where and Who

So what to do about abundance? In summary, the secret is to attract it into our lives. In order to do that, we have to go deep within ourselves until we reach our innermost point of complete stillness Then we will behold "abundance" in all its glory.

And when we return to the world outside, will be magically all around us. This is our duty in life. This best way to help ourselves and our fellow earth citizens is by discovering the secret of abundance. Our true path is to find abundance for all people and for all of nature's creatures.

In that well of discovery, we can all drink to our heart's content. The secret map to reach the state of abundance is cleverly concealed, perhaps as a test of our intelligence, in our most useful faculty called "Mind."

The Author

Selwyn Gishen is the author of "Mind," a selection of some of the unique teachings that he learned from his mentor, Kavi Yogiraj Mani Finger.

For the past 40 years, Selwyn studied and practiced the philosophy and techniques necessary to align personal mind patterns with the goals and objectives of human endeavor. By aligning personal endeavors with one's individual mind patterns, one can become a magnet for all that one desires.

Many people suffer from the inability to direct their lives in a way that can produce harmony and at the same time attract abundance. Abundance, in this context, is the level of awareness at which one finds oneself in loving relationships, with sufficient material comforts, fulfilling careers and the experience of an overall level of joy and happiness.

Life can be joyful although it often seems like a roller coaster ride, with many ups and downs. "Mind" offers a philosophy and a practical step by step guide to help change those patterns of thinking that have not produced results in the way one had hoped they would. By changing one's perspective and keying into a natural flow of energy, life becomes easier than a mere struggle for survival.

We learn to live life. Life is an experience of real joy - not a hedonistic palace of temporary pleasure. Life is meant to be the true experience of a deep soul stirring wonder that is full of meaning and purpose.

We have never been taught the art of creating abundance or even how to experience happiness. When we are happy, very few issues are too bothersome. When we are happy, we are in the best mental state of mind to solve problems. Happiness is infectious. When we are happy, we can make others happy too.

My goal is to help you to find that place of abundance where happiness and joy reign supreme and wealth means having lots of health, wealth, wisdom, love and freedom.

Selwyn studied directly with his mentor, Kavi Yogiraj Mani Finger (see Tribute). He learned many practical techniques to set up mental patterns to bring about a more tranquil, focused state of living. This book is an introduction to some of those techniques

A Tribute to Kavi Yogiraj Mani Finger

The Kavi, was a world authority on the subject of meditation and techniques that promote life fulfilling experiences. He was consulted by thousands of people from all walks of life. From religious ministers to prime ministers, from doctors to teachers, from regular folks to the most successful corporate leaders; they all came for his wisdom and knowledge regarding ways to develop a successful mode of thinking and behavior that would permeate all aspects of their life.

No matter how successful his clients were in their own particular fields of expertise, they always returned again and again to learn from a "life master." Many were plagued with serious illness, some terminal; others had difficult personal relationships, most were seeking a better lifestyle and to all of them he offered a way to find the Truth and to understand their Reality so they could grow and prosper as humans.

The Kavi never wrote any books but he gave many

lectures that were recorded on tape. Many were transcribed into notes. Much of what he knew and taught was passed on directly, on a one to one basis. Many spiritual practitioners and teachers from all over the world came to visit the Kavi, many traveling thousands of miles to see him and to participate with him in forums concerning self realization and personal growth. He was even nominated as the President of WHO (World Health Organization) for the year of 1969.

His greatest achievement though, was his own personal development. After being mandated to serve in the military during World War II by the South African government, he returned home shell shocked and desperately ill. The Kavi though, as good fortune would have it, was introduced to certain special spiritual and personal growth techniques during a visit to Los Angeles in the late 1950's.

It was there that he met the famous Indian saint, Paramahansa Yogananda, (founder of the Self Realization Institute) and was instructed in ways of meditation and breath control that had been taught and practiced for thousands of years in India and by mystics around the world - techniques that had stood the test of time and were on the cutting edge of spiritual development, personal growth and realization.

The Kavi brought this knowledge back to South

Africa where he then set up a school and foundation to help people discover the 'path of abundance'. He pioneered ways to teach these techniques to a western audience regardless of their faith or cultural heritage. His techniques appealed to people of all cultures and ethnic groups.

The Kavi himself became living proof of a person who achieved the abundant life. He was abundantly healthy and totally cured of his shell shocked condition. He had more devoted students than any other spiritual and life teacher in South Africa. He had followers in England, France, Germany and Australia. He taught men, women and children all that he knew so they would lead better and more fulfilled lives.

Most of all he taught and practiced love. People who came into his presence felt his love and were healed by it. Most especially, they became more loving and joyful within their own hearts.

The Kavi passed away in July 2002, in Boca Raton, Florida at the young age of ninety two. He was a mental giant till the day of his passing. He managed to live an incredible life of accomplishment and fulfillment. His legacy will live on.

www.ingramcontent.com/pod-product-compliance
Lightning Source LLC
Chambersburg PA
CBHW032100080426
42733CB00006B/354